"Who'll Bring Me Flowers?"

by
Anita A. Rozzi

RoseDog Books
PITTSBURGH, PENNSYLVANIA 15238

RoseDog Books
585 Alpha Drive, Suite 103
Pittsburgh, PA 15238
Visit our website at *www.rosedogbookstore.com*

ISBN: 979-8-88729-114-7
eISBN: 979-8-88729-614-2

WHO WILL BRING ME FLOWERS

This manuscript is written primarily for my three children. In recalling the events of my childhood that ultimately formed me into the adult that I became, it is not my intension to create an impression that one of my family was less, or more, guilty than another for what transpired in our lives. Each of us is capable of inflicting pain on our own. My family was no exception. It's just that we seemed to be particularly adept at it.

Encouraged by my daughter, I have attempted to recount as accurately as possible the events as they occurred and the impact that they still have on my life. Some of the memories recalled here have been suppressed for many years and have surfaced only recently. In some instances this has had an effect comparable to touching my tongue to a tooth ache that had finally stopped hurting only to start the throbbing again. Other memories have caused me to relive some pleasant, nostalgic moments of times past and happily recalled.

Hopefully, the finished product will serve as a catharsis for me. Perhaps after reading it my children will better understand some of my own parental failures and be able to benefit from my experiences.

At the very least, I hope they will enjoy the journey of walking through my childhood and some of my adult years with me.

*"Is there a land beyond the stars
Where we may find eternal day,
Life after death, Peace after wars?
Is there? I cannot say.
Shall we find a happier life,
All joy that here we never know,
Love in all things, an end to strife?
Perhaps: It may be so."*

—Thomas Wolfe

To Linda, Mike and Jim (Gov).
Each of you are a book in yourselves, living testimony
of three times that I got it right
and the reason I draw my next breath.

This is for you with love.

FORWARD

The room was quiet now. The angry voices grown hoarse from shouting had stopped and been replaced by muffled sobs which she realized were her own. She took her hands from over her ears in time to hear the door slam. She knew that Dad had put on his wide brimmed, white hat and left the house…a clear indication that she was still vulnerable.

She hugged Mother Cat tightly to her thin chest hoping that the responding, raspy purr would not disclose their hiding place.

Very early in life, experience had taught her that the calm that seemed to prevail was only temporary and that the furor would resume again before this day was over. She would wait here crouched under the kitchen table until Mother was occupied at the stove. Then she would make her escape out the back door, race barefoot with Mother Cat sprinting ahead to the barn where Dad would be milking the Jersey cow, Beauty.

When he had finished stripping the last few drops of milk from the young heifer's teats she would follow him as he carried the bucket of foamy milk to the small shed that housed the cream separator. Together they would crank the machine that would separate the cream from the whey. Then they would carry the buckets to the house. Later they would churn the cream into butter but tonight the warm, weak milk would be poured over pieces of bread and become their evening meal.

She walked closer to him than usual occasionally causing the milk to slosh over the rim of the bucket as she brushed against his leg while attempting to match his long stride.

As they neared the house he stepped aside creating a space between the two of them and she knew this was his way of avoiding the appearance of showing affection for her which inevitably would rekindle the quarreling and anger she had just witnessed.

"Are we going in now?"

"Just stay out of their way." He responded.

She was four years old.

HOW WE BEGAN

My dad was the eighth child born into a family of eleven children. His parents moved from their native state of Kentucky to Texas when he was a relatively young boy. There he completed his early education. After high school he worked his way through college and earned degrees in Teaching, Child Psychology and School Management and Administration. He taught at numerous schools there and at one time coached a girl's high school basketball team.

He made his first trip to New Mexico Territory in 1911 when he was twenty three years old and was so impressed by the wide open spaces and Gamma Grass that was stirrup high while riding on horseback that he made a determination to settle there after completing his teaching obligations in Texas.

These plans were delayed when the U.S. entered World War I. After serving a three or four year hitch in the Infantry where he taught some of his fellow soldiers to read and write he returned to Texas for more years of teaching in the public schools.

It was while teaching in one of these small high schools that he met my mother, a petite, dark haired, dark eyed girl sixteen years his junior and a student in one of his classes. They were married the day after she graduated high school.

In the spring of 1927 their first child was born. She was a large, demanding, noisy but strikingly pretty baby with wide blue eyes and dark curly hair. They named her Nadine.

Dad was determined to pursue his dream of farming on the land he had claimed utilizing the terms of The Homestead Act. So in the spring of that year, after instructing my mother that their baby must not be allowed to cry for want of attention, he loaded his twenty-three year old wife, their baby, who was crying, and their few belongings into his Model-T Ford and set out to begin a new life. He was thirty-nine years old.

This is as good a place as any to note that in spite of the emphasis and care taken to prevent it, Nadine managed to turn crying into an art form and utilize its benefits throughout our life together.

Mother, who had always enjoyed favorite child status in her family of two brothers and a sister had never lived outside the state of Texas and was immediately struck by the flat, dry plains that greeted them as they drove West toward their destination.

Dad had sent his military pay home to his parents who had, with his two younger brothers and sister and their families, preceded him to New Mexico. He had assumed that his earnings would be kept in trust by his parents so he would have a nest egg to help him get established once he was discharged. One can only imagine his disappointment when upon returning home he learned that the money had instead been used to send his sister to college and help his brothers start up their farms.

So instead of the family home he had planned on building, their first home was a small two room house twelve feet by twenty-four feet with four windows, a front and back door and floors of rough, hewn wood, with no electricity or running water and the conventional out-house a few yards away. This was a grim contrast to the six room home with a wrap-around porch sheltered by shade and pecan trees that Mother had left behind.

Immature, homesick and unaccustomed to the hard work she was exposed to, Mother never really adjusted to this lifestyle. She frequently referred to her surroundings as "This God forsaken place." Over seventy years later, old and with memory of recent events murky she could clearly remember her happier childhood and still called Texas 'home'.

Dad acquired a team of work horses by catching two wild ones and breaking them to work a plow. According to notes made by my mother, their first harvested crop produced five one-hundred pound bags of Pinto beans. The going price per hundred pound bag was around five dollars.

He continued teaching school for a year or so in New Mexico, but farming had become a passion so he went on to break-out more land and plant more crops. Planting time was determined by frequent referrals to the Farmer's Almanac and testing the moisture of the soil by scooping his hand a few inches into the ground to check how much of the winter snow had penetrated the ground.

Provision for water for our use as well as for that of the livestock was done by hauling water from a large storage tank several miles from the house. A tubular shaped tank of corrugated medal was mounted on the bed of the old truck and could hold several hundred gallons of water. Dad would pull alongside the large open tank and dip and pour bucket after bucket of water into the round opening at the front of the tank on the truck. When it was full he placed a fitted lid into the small opening and drove the laden truck back home. By removing the stopper at the lower end of the tank water could be released into a galvanized tub for the cattle. This tank once nearly became a medal tomb for me as a result of a foolish game of dare initiated by Nadine.

Tenacious and seemingly tireless, Dad continued to enlarge his fields until he eventually had several hundred acres of cultivated land.

He was able to acquire a bull, a few head of Jersey milk cows, some white faced cattle for beef and a small herd of sheep. Mother told repeated stories of trying to round-up these incredibly stupid creatures while carrying their hefty, crying, two year old toddler straddling her hip.

Throughout the ensuing months and years he added several outbuildings. A barn with milking stalls and storage area for feed was made using railroad ties. He built a house of slab rock where we hung our hams to cure and sides of beef to keep cold in the winter months. A half dug-out with a corrugated metal roof was located a few feet east of this building. This was a sturdy, fairly large structure but I always had a feeling of claustrophobia whenever I was in it in spite of the south windows above ground that let in plenty of light. There was a damp, musty odor inside and I imagined little four legged creatures scurrying around in the shadows when I was sent down there on an errand. The addition of these outbuildings was necessary and improved the overall operation of work functions but nothing was done to enlarge our house. When we sold the farm in 1941 six of us were sharing the crowded space in our small two room home.

A NO GOOD WIND

The early 1930's ushered in the era that came to be known as the Great Depression. Banks closed. Suicides as a result of the Stock Market crash became common place. Bread lines formed along city streets that a short time ago had been alive with prospers shoppers.

Particularly hard hit was the American farmer. Not because they lost money due to the bank closures-they had very little to begin with, but because Mother Nature chose this time to unleash her fury in the form of the Dust Bowl. Following a severe drought, land that had been over-grazed and over-farmed lay vulnerable and easy victim to the weathers wrath.

Corn that had been planted in the spring failed to mature due to lack of rain. Row after row of grey-green stalks stood in fields like withered skeletons. Dwarfed sugar cane intended to be used for cattle feed leaned with tassels bowed as if in prayer-or defeat. Hungry cattle grew lank as pastures dried up.

And dust was everywhere. It moved across the land like a blanket of red fog propelled by a wind that never relented.

Day and night the wind blew. The sun was shrouded during the day with a pink-red haze. At night Mother pinned sheets from the top of the metal head rails to the foot of the bed in an attempt to shield us from inhaling the dust during our sleep.

Dust. Worn like a cosmetic, there simply was no avoiding it.

Hellfire and Brimstone preachers took to their pulpits to announce that God's wrath as foretold in the book of Revelation had fallen upon mankind and few, if any, had tenable evidence to doubt it. As if to further validate their prophecy of doom, grass fires caused by static electricity from the wind swept through miles of land destroying pastures, followed by a massive invasion of army worms that ravaged the tender bean sprouts struggling to survive.

Though the land was deemed barren, the same could not be said of its tenants. Large families seemed to abound. More hungry mouths around a table set with meager portions became the norm.

This was the world into which I made my appearance in the very early hours of a cold March morning. "Blown in by a No Good Wind." I was told.

Considering the wretchedness of the times, it's no wonder that my arrival gave little cause for celebration, I suppose, but my sister was the most upset by my entrance into what she considered to be her world to rule.

Nadine was one month shy of her third birthday when I was born. Dad had taken her to his brother's house the night before and brought my aunt back home with him to assist in my delivery. Mother wrote that the following morning when he picked her up he told her there was a surprise waiting for her at home.

"Does it have a white face?" She asked.

"Yes." Dad said.

"Does it have red hair?"

Again, "Yes."

Believing me to be the white faced calf Dad had promised to give her someday, Nadine was ecstatic on the way home.

I'm told that upon seeing me lying next to our mother she began frantically tugging at the blankets in an attempt to rid herself of someone whom she perceived to be an intruder into her rightful place. The neighbor woman who came to help out until Mother was back on her feet constantly had to be alert and watchful to prevent her from harming me and was confronted with a challenge she wasn't expecting.

Demanding and precocious, Nadine had quickly learned that throwing herself on the floor in an outburst of kicking and sobbing was an effective method of getting her way. It is difficult to understand why Dad, a student and teacher of child psychology had allowed her behavior to become so out of control. But this was one study in human behavior that had gotten past him. At age three she had firmly established control over our family. Throughout our lives every major family decision was made with the overriding concern being one of how she would react to it.

She never outgrew these displays of temper as she grew older but merely replaced them with a more subtle and often cruel method of expression.

MY father was a brilliant, hardworking man. But the strongest personalities have their impotent side and he despised a "commotion" so rather than confronting this negative behavior and taking corrective action, he chose instead to ignore and avoid it by leaving the house and plunge into his work which in itself must have seemed overwhelming.

Still, he managed to eke out an existence. Meat was derived from butchering a cow or hog, often skin and bones themselves. Every scrap of meat was stripped from the bones and canned in quart fruit jars in order to preserve it for future use and then only in sparingly small amounts as one quart might need to be spread over several meals. Usually he was able to purchase a few pounds of flour or corn meal for bread. The corn meal was sometimes boiled in water to make "mush" which served as the evening meal on more than one occasion. To this day the sight of a bowl of Cream of Wheat can make my stomach lurch.

DONELLA

In the early summer of 1932 a new baby arrived in our family. Another girl.

According to Mother's notes she was a beautiful baby with dark curly hair and dark eyes. They named her Donella.

That winter and spring of the following year were particularly severe. Our little house had been built using green lumber and when it dried out it left large cracks between the floor boards and around the windows that let in the cold air.

The three of became ill with sore throats that developed into tonsillitis and high fevers. The nearest town with a doctor was forty-five miles from where we lived and was considered as being quite a distance in those days. Even so, Dad drove us in to town where he rented a room in a spinster's home in order to be near medical help. No antibiotics or so called 'wonder drugs' were in existence at that time. Basically a country doctor's remedy of Vicks rubs and keeping the covers piled on causing us to overheat and sweat thereby breaking the fever was the general treatment.

Being the smallest and least resistant to infection, Donella was stricken with Dust Pneumonia and died a few months short of her first birthday.

She was buried in a small country cemetery where both my parents rest today. The area was desolate and barren as was most of the land everywhere and Mother lamented years later that they had to leave her on the prairie in this "God Forsaken Land."

The loss of this child exacerbated Mother's depression and discontent. Nadine and I were of no comfort. We were six and three years old. We could not comprehend either death or our mother's frequent outbursts and rather than draw closer we quarreled among ourselves which only made matters worse.

Nadine had become accustomed to dominating Mother's attention and now finding it withheld, she became more abusive toward me. With no place else to turn I would run to the field barefoot to register a complaint with Dad. Frustrated and overworked he would give me a brief hearing and send me back to the house after sternly instructing me to "Stay out of their way!"

Sandwiched between a larger, aggressive older sister who had been conditioned to having her way and Mother's frustration which she sometimes expressed by a slap to the side of the head, I grew more timid and withdrawn. In my quest to find the safety of "Out-of Their-Way", I sought the comfort of my companion, Mother Cat and the security of our hiding place under the kitchen table. In later years Mother once remarked to one of her friend that "Anita is always so quiet. We never know she is on the place." I was there. I had become an insignificant, invisible presence caught in the eye of a perpetually brewing storm.

Lacking in self- discipline and natural maternal instincts, Mother frequently left the two of us alone and walked to the field where Dad was working to announce that she was going back 'home' and he could "just keep these damned kids." On each occasion Dad would stop his work long enough to calm her down, bring her back to the house, check that we were alright and return to the field where he would work past dark.

With money scarce and receiving little support from his mate, these interruptions and delays must have been especially discouraging.

This is in no way intended to imply that Mother did not work hard because she did. Her knuckles were rough and red from scrubbing our clothes-everything from sheets to heavy work overalls on a medal scrub board in a galvanized tub filled with hot water and strong homemade lye soap. In the winter sometimes these clothes would freeze to the line before she finished hanging them out. She cooked three meals a day on a wood burning stove and worked in the field when Dad was short of help.

Essentially, I think that what she had envisioned was going to be an extended, adventurous honeymoon had instead resulted in disillusionment and disappointment for her. By marrying Dad who was much older perhaps she had expected that she would always be someone's 'little girl' and faced with what she perceived as competition from her own children she became bitter and resentful.

THE NEW TRACTOR

By 1934 the winds had begun to cease somewhat but history would later record this year as having been the worst drought year in U.S. history.

Many farmers had abandoned their land to seek a better life by moving further west. Those that stayed on continued to work their fields.

By borrowing against his next crop Dad was able to purchase a new tractor and enough bean and corn seed to start a new crop.

The day the tractor was delivered to our farm was one of heightened excitement. A cloud of dust in the distance and the loud pop-pop of the engine signaled that it was on its way to our place.

Soon enough the bright green piece of equipment with the equally bright yellow letters spelling out the name John Deere emblazoned on both sides of the engine was clearly visible. It was a mighty machine with giant iron spiked wheels and puffs of black smoke belching from the exhaust pipe. Farmers often referred to this brand of tractor as 'Poppin' Johnny' due to the staccato popping of the engine.

Mother had come to the door of the house upon hearing the commotion. When she saw Dad inspecting the tractor she burst into tears and retreated back inside.

Later that night I was awakened by her crying loudly and yelling that it had been four years since she had been home to visit her folks and if he could afford that damned tractor, why couldn't he afford her a trip 'home'

I pulled the covers over my head to avoid hearing the argument which carried on into the night.

After breakfast the next morning Dad filled up its tank with kerosene, turned the huge fly wheel with a great swing of his arms and instantly the engine responded with the rhythmic popping again. Seeing me watching nearby, he motioned me to come near. As he climbed onto the seat he reached down, lifted me up to sit between his knees and we were off to try out this magnificent piece of equipment. Needless to say there was hell to pay when we returned later sunburned and covered with dust.

Mother was waiting in the yard grim faced and angry with Nadine clutching her skirt. As we drew nearer, Nadine began to stamp her feet (crying).

"I'm supposed to be first!" "I'm supposed to be first!" She detached herself from Mothers skirt and ran to Dad, hugged his leg and began crying more loudly.

Feigning calm, yet furious, Mother faced Dad. She announced resolutely and without raising her voice that because of this tractor we would no doubt be in debt for the rest of our lives. Even so, debt or no debt, she was going 'home' even if she had to walk to the main road and catch a ride and he could have his damned tractor and all that went with it.

The arguing and crying continued for some time but I was oblivious to it as I hurried to the barn in search of Mother Cat so I could share this wonderful experience with her.

Even now the thrill of sharing that first ride with my Dad is a memory that I treasure.

Mother didn't have to make good her threat to hitch a ride 'home'. That fall we harvested a crop that was profitable enough to allow us to buy a fairly late model car and make the trip to Texas.

I MEET MY GRANDPARENTS

I was four years old when I remember visiting my maternal grandparents, Grandma and Grandpa Brown and Mother's youngest brother Halstead for the first time. He was a tall, slim man with warm mischievous brown eyes and a contagious smile. I became his shadow while we were there. His wife, Willie, was small and soft spoken. They had been sweethearts as children and the love they felt for each other filled any room they were in. They lived with my grandparents and had no children. The three of us bonded instantly and that bond remained strong until the time of their deaths.

Grandpa was also tall. Being of Irish heritage he had blue eyes, red hair turning white and fair skin. He had spent his youth in Tennessee and still spoke with the drawl peculiar to that region of the country with 'r's sounding like 'ah's.

I was his first grandchild born with red hair for which he took the credit and he made no attempt to hide his favoritism which naturally did not put me in good standing with his other grandchildren.

I was immediately taken by the contrast between his farm and ours-cotton growing in rich black earth versus pinto beans in sandstone colored soil; a large cow barn with a loft and sectioned stalls for milking and tree after tree loaded with peaches and still green pecans.

There was a creek that ran behind the house and at night the sounds of croaking frogs lulled us to sleep.

After dark he would take me out on the long porch where we would sit in cane-bottom rocking chairs and he would point to the tiny flickering lights in the shrubbery and explain the mysteries of fire flies. Those visits with him had a surreal, magical effect and I never wanted them to end.

Grandma, on the other hand was his exact opposite. She was olive skinned and of mixed Cherokee heritage with grey hair and flashing black eyes. She was tiny in stature but a ball of fire by nature. Her face was lined with thousands of wrinkles and she wore her hair pulled back in a tight bun. She wore floor length dark, cotton print dresses, thick black cotton stockings and sensible black lace-up shoes. Her apron which could be converted into a basket for gathering eggs also had a pocket that held a small tin of snuff which she refilled from time to time from a ribbed glass container with a Garrett Snuff label. These glasses were washed and used for table glasses when they became empty. Periodically she would take a small twig which at one time had belonged on a willow tree but now having pulled off the bark and chewed one end into the likeness of a small brush, it was an ideal utensil to dip into the tin and extract just the right amount of snuff to tuck under her tongue. I learned soon enough not to stand too close when she had taken a fresh dip because inevitably she would begin to talk before it dissolved and emit little puffs of brown powder which burned like fire if it got in your eyes.

She was a small, spunky little woman with a somewhat sour disposition and I tended to shy away from her even when she let me help her gather the eggs at the end of the day.

Neither Grandpa nor Grandma had teeth and when they chewed their cheeks puffed out and their eyes looked scrunched up. I hoped that when I got old that my teeth wouldn't disappear.

A LESSON TO LEARN

A few days after we arrived, Grandpa hitched two of his mules to his wagon for a trip to the town three miles away to pick up a supply of groceries. We could have gone in our car, but Grandpa said this would be "a good lesson."

The wagon had two wooden benches that went the width of the wagon. There was no overhead covering and the hot Texas sun bore down on us without mercy.

We creaked slowly down the narrow road that had deep ruts and black mud puddles left from a recent rain.

We passed cotton fields with Negroes bent under the weight of long heavy canvas sacks, picking cotton. Their shanty type houses setting back from the road was a testament to their abject poverty. Some of these workers were mere children no older than I and they looked up briefly as we passed by. I had never seen a black person before and waved at these 'different' little people. I was rewarded with a sharp slap on my wrist by Grandma who sternly informed me that "We do not speak to Coloreds!"

When we arrived at the store, I saw more Blacks leaning against the wall outside the building. My childish curiosity got the best of me again and I hung back to stare up at these dark-skinned people with tight curly hair. Again, Grandma was quick to notice my dallying and took me roughly by the arm and guided me into the store ahead of her.

We bought a supply of groceries and several glasses of snuff. Grandpa took me to a variety store down the street that had a candy case containing a mixture of different candies. He gave me a nickel and I bought a nice sized bag of mixed chocolates.

This store had a water fountain on one wall. Over it was a large sign with the words "WHITES ONLY" printed on it. I wondered what terrible thing these

"Coloreds" had done that they should be denied a drink of water.

Childlike, I soon forgot their troubles when we climbed back upon the wagon to go home. On the trip back I sat between Grandpa and Dad on the front bench and soon dozed off unmindful that the hot sun was doing a job on the chocolates in my bag.

After the chores were done that afternoon, Uncle Halstead took us to a ditch that held a deep puddle and showed us some tadpoles wriggling around in the muddy water. He gave us a jar and let us slip off our shoes and step into the ditch to catch some of these slinky little creatures.

Our mission completed, we climbed back onto the bank with our catch and began our walk to the house for supper.

Only a few paces up the road and still barefooted, my legs and feet were suddenly struck with a stinging pain that made me cry out and dance from one foot to the other.

"CHIGGERS"!

No amount of scrubbing with soap and water could ease this burning and itching torment. At length, Grandma had us put our feet in a pan and she rubbed corn syrup over our ankles and feet. Only then did the pain subside and although I hated the sticky mess, I was grateful for the relief.

Grandpa had been right. This day had indeed been a lesson. I had my first glimpse into the suffering brought about by human discrimination and the dichotomy of my own suffering caused by indiscriminate insects.

At least my misery was of short duration.

We spent the rest of our time visiting with other relatives. Each house was warm and inviting and the tables were loaded with good country cooking. There were lots of cousins and different games to play.

All too soon, it seemed, our visit was over and it was time to leave. As Dad was loading our things back in the car, Uncle Halstead took me by the hand and walked over to him and asked, "Why don't you just let us keep Anita?"

Without turning around, Dad said, "Well, you might as well. She's not going to amount to much anyway."

My heart leaped with excitement. I could stay! I squeezed my Uncles hand tightly and waited for Dad to start sorting my things from the packed bags. Instead, he picked me up under the arms and set me roughly in the back seat and closed the door.

He shook hands with Uncle Halstead, waited for Mother to say her tearful goodbyes and we pulled away. With tears streaming down my cheeks, I looked out the rear window and waved to Uncle Halstead who was waving back. I was not accustomed to this type of adult teasing and it took some time before I re-covered-if, indeed, I ever really did.

We stopped for an overnight visit with two of Dad's sisters who lived in West Texas. They each lived in large frame houses with big rooms. The front room was considered to be a parlor and only used when company came. Al-though it was very nicely furnished and walled with pretty paper, the room itself was not heated and in colder weather we spent our time in a room in the center of the house which had a fireplace that took up one entire wall.

The cousins here were much older than we were. Most of them were school teachers, so all the talk was very grown-up and serious. Life seemed to be taken very seriously here and we children were all but invisible.

It was not hard to leave these places.

I have no actual recollection of my grandmother Austin but photographs of her show her to be a tall, slender very dignified, unsmiling woman. I'm told that she was extremely hard working and that even though she was almost totally blind, kept an immaculate house.

Grandpa Austin, who survived her death, was also tall and slender and distant by nature. He had very fair skin, high cheek bones and cold blue eyes. His occa-sional visits to us were brief and generally not very comfortable ones. He was a firm believer that children should keep their place and that was not necessarily in the company of adults.

He was a devotedly religious man and his prayer of grace before each meal was, at least from a child's prospective, long enough to cause one to grow faint from hunger.

He had been a farmer by trade also but I never saw him when he wasn't dressed as though he was on his way to church.

I don't believe I ever had a one sentence conversation with him and he didn't encourage one but occasionally he would reach into the pocket of his suit jacket and take out a small brown bag with the top neatly turned down in small folds.

Meticulously he would unfold the bag and let me reach in for a piece of candy. It was always small hard pieces of horehound. I didn't particularly like the bitter taste but it was, after all, candy.

He remarried a small, plump widow woman when he was eighty one years old. She had been widowed for some time and was quiet and soft spoken and had a much warmer personality than he did and asked us to refer to her as 'Auntie'. She also preceded him in death.

Grandpa Austin died peacefully in his sleep at the age of eighty eight years eight months and eight days old.

Throughout the years we repeated the trips back to Texas from time to time and I looked forward to each visit with my Grandparents and Uncle and Aunt.

On one occasion Uncle Halstead had a job as a mail carrier on a rural route. He always took me with him in his Model-A car and let me put the mail in the boxes. He had a story to tell about each family on the route.

He and Aunt Willie took me to a Picture Show in town. These times were as close to my being spoiled as I will ever know in this life.

Late in their marriage they had a daughter of their own and named her after me. But by then I was an adult and had started my own family so I never had the opportunity to cultivate a close relationship with her but Uncle Halstead, Aunt Willie and I communicated regularly until the time of their death.

Uncle Halstead developed Parkinson Disease and passed away at age seventy-eight. As is often the case when two souls and hearts are so closely entwined, Aunt Willie soon followed him.

The two of them were the only people in my young life who had shown any affection or love toward me and their passing left a void in my life that I feel to this day.

Both of my grandparents lived to be almost a hundred years old.

WE GROW AGAIN

This particular trip 'home' must have restored some sense of tranquility into our house however temporary, because in May of that year Mother gave birth to a fourth child, another girl. This baby had very blond hair, big blue eyes and was thin and frail.

Having so recently lost a child, her seemingly fragile appearance prompted the folks to take an especially protective attitude toward her. The slightest whimper brought us all to her side. Mother 'nursed' her many times throughout the day in an attempt to "build her up".

They named her Leola, a name she disliked so much that in her adult years she referred to herself as "Lee" and insisted that we all do the same.

In spite of her delicate appearance Lee was as healthy and energetic as the rest of us. As she grew older she and I became great playmates. We were 'Mothers' with our dolls and visited each other in our playhouses. We made mud pies decorated with sprigs of weeds and baked them in the heat of the sun-even daring each other to take a taste.

We invented great imaginary characters renaming ourselves Anna and Lou, girl detectives. We solved many mysterious crimes conceived from our reading the Nancy Drew books.

We raced barefoot down dusty roads rolling old tires (our cars) hot on the trail of counterfeiters (whatever that was).

On the first day of school when Lee was five or six years old, Dad turned to me as he dropped us off in front of the building and said, "Take care of your sister," an assignment which I may have taken too seriously.

On the school ground if I even perceived that she was being mistreated I was there to deal with the offender, sometimes with unfortunate results for myself.

I recall that once when she was made to sit at her desk through recess, I refused to go to the playground but sat on the school steps until the bell rang.

My role as intercessor and protector lasted well into our adult years and was not always necessary or appreciated by her. I took on a maternal instinct where she was concerned and she would take offense at times.

As we took separate roads in our lives after leaving home we seemed to have less and less in common and when my position of rescuer from her failed marriages, abusive husbands, and financial set-backs became a means of resentment by her, we eventually stopped communicating altogether.

THE THREE ROOM SCHOOL HOUSE

Dad became a farmer by trade but never gave up his inherent ability to teach. He was never too tired or busy to sit with us and teach us new things. He had retained some materials from his classroom days; McGuffy Readers , an arithmetic book or two, and a small set of encyclopedias that he had purchased through a Readers Digest subscription.   The books were small, bound in red cloth and we handled them with much care.

A great fabric wall map that rolled up on a spring cylinder much like the ones on a window shade, hung near the ceiling in the kitchen. On the rare occasions that he unrolled it to show us locations of the countries we were studying, it covered almost the entire wall.

This map would be considered a real treasure today but as with so many other things during that time, its potential future value was unrecognized and we did not keep it when we moved from that house years later.

In the evenings after supper he would pull three chairs up to the kitchen table and with Nadine on one side and me on the other he would teach us the rudiments of reading using the dim light of the kerosene lamp. I'm not sure about this, but again taken from Mother's notes, I could read quite fluently by the age of two and a half years old.

On occasion he would make a trip to town where the county had a small book depository. He would bring back several reading books. There was Aesop's Fables, all with moral endings. The Man The Boy and The Donkey, The Ant and the Grasshopper, and two of my favorites, The Shoemaker and the Elves and The Town Mouse and The Country Mouse. As we grew older there were the Louisa Mae Alcott books; Eight Cousins, Rose in Bloom and the Little Women series. Then there were the Elsie Densmore books. Was it really possible that one little girl could be so perfect and yet so misunderstood?

School was ten miles from home and in the same vicinity as two General Stores. It was a three room building with several classes taught in each room. It was constructed with a grey cement exterior and was most likely built by WPA workers. Each room was heated with a pot- bellied coal burning stove with a stove pipe extending through the ceiling. It was not uncommon for birds to nest in the uncovered openings in the summer so the first fire in the winter usually resulted in the rooms becoming full of black smoke because of the blocked chimney. We were evacuated to stand outside in the cold until the room cleared enough to allow us to return to the classroom.

The playground was dirt that had been graded smooth and hard. There was a slide, a swing set made with metal pipes and wooden seats and a basketball court which the boys claimed as their inherent, exclusive territory. This was their place to shoot hoops, or if the ball had gone flat from lack of air, to spin their homemade wooden tops on the hard surface. If a girl dared to cross over the line that marked its boundary, she was immediately surrounded and told that if she did it again they would pull her underpants off and hang them from one of the hoops. This was an excellent deterrent. In the seven years of attendance there I never saw bloomers flapping from the basketball hoops.

There were two outhouses behind the main building, one marked Boys and the other Girls.

This was pretty much the lay out of my first formal institution of learning.

Certain enrollment requirements were necessary in order to justify hiring three teachers and the school was a number of students short of meeting that requirement. The County School Superintendent who knew Dad approached him and appealed to him to enroll me. He knew I was under age so he stressed that I would not actually need to participate in class but just be registered as part of the head count in first grade and Dad consented.

Nadine entered third grade that year and was in a different classroom than I was. She was considered to be very bright and did well in school.

My first teacher was a young woman with long, chestnut brown hair and large doe eyes.

It has been said that the impact a child's first teacher has on her students can last throughout their school years and beyond. Marie Lamb proved this to be true. She took an interest in me and had a positive influence on decisions I would make long after I was no longer her student.

Her classroom was furnished with a long blackboard on one wall with three or four erasers. Her large desk faced a dozen or so smaller wooden desks with polished tops that had a hole to accommodate an ink well and a hollowed out groove to hold a pencil. These desks were arranged in three or four rows with an isle between each row.

Brightly painted shelves made from rough lumber held books and supplies which were all furnished by the State.

A sand box on legs filled with clean white sand was located in one corner to provide amusement in the event bad weather prevented us from going outdoors during recess.

Alphabet blocks, modeling clay, which often became grimy from being dropped in the sand box, Math and Spelling Flash Cards, a tall jar of white paste and a few boxes of colored crayons completed the furnishings.

Each student was given a Big Chief writing tablet with rough pages. The red cover bore a picture of someone's impression of an Indian Chief complete with headdress.

We were allowed one lead pencil made of cedar with a pointed eraser that broke off the first time it was used. The pencil smelled wonderful but when sharpened, it tore the brittle pages of the tablet.

Our lesson assignments were produced on a gel hectograph. The master sheet was written with a special indelible lead pencil or ink then placed face down on a tray similar in size to an eight by ten cookie sheet containing gel. When the original paper was removed an impression was left on the pad. Copies were made by using a roller to press blank papers onto the gelatin mat. Each time a copy was made some of the ink was removed from the gelatin and after fifty or so copies they were successively lighter and more difficult to read.

Teachers were respected and supported for the most part by our parents and had their work cut out for them. They taught several different classes in the same room and maintained discipline. A far cry from today's disorderly, over-crowded classrooms.

In addition to being graded on scholastic merit, equal importance was placed on the grade we were given in deportment. A minor infraction of the rules cost you recess time. You stayed indoors with your head down on the desk. A more serious breech earned you a crack across the palm of your hand with a ruler. Even paddle boards were used, though rarely.

But discipline did not end when the last bell rang. Get in trouble at school-expect double trouble when you got home.

KENNY AND THE READING LESSON

On my first day of school I was assigned to sit next to Kenny Saline. He was a German boy with a shaved head and a perpetual scowl on his face. This was his second year in first grade.

Miss Lamb gave each of us a thin reading book with a picture of a smiling boy and girl on the cover and short stories in bold type print.

Since I was not considered to be a student, she told me I could just look at the pictures while Kenny read.

Using his index finger to point to each word, Kenny began. Sadly, he knew letters but not words and had to spell each word aloud for Miss Lamb to pronounce for him.

Having become familiar with reading the books Dad had brought home which were far more advanced than this primmer book, his stumbling annoyed me terribly.

Exasperated, I began to read aloud over his spelling. "Happy was a dog. Happy liked to run. Happy liked to jump. Happy said bow-wow."

I was to regret this braggadocio impulse. At recess Kenny cornered me and grabbing my arm in both hands, wrung the flesh on my wrist so hard I could not hold back my tears.

Over supper that evening I announced with a great deal of determination that I would not be returning to "that dumb school."

When asked for an explanation, I'm told that my answer was that I had been made to sit next to Kenny and he didn't know Happy from bow-wow!

The next day Dad spoke to the teacher and asked if I could use a more advanced reader. She agreed, moved me over to the next row of desks and there I stayed for the remainder of the year.

I was four years old and in the second grade. I avoided Kenny like the plague.

I delighted in my elevated academic status as a second grader and was eager to learn whatever came my way.

The school day always began by each of us standing by our desk and reciting a verse from the Bible. I prided myself in memorizing and quoting various verses rather than the oft repeated first verse of the Twenty Third Psalm. I never understood why the Lord would want us to "lie down in green pastures" anyway.

But if I excelled in the classroom, I was a miserable failure on the playground. I stood in scruffy contrast to the other girls who were relatively well groomed and wore a different dress almost every day. We had three dresses. Two were for school, each worn two days in sequence and one for Sunday school. Often at least one of these dresses, with matching bloomers, would have been made from printed cotton flour sacks. Our school shoes were coarse and usually in need of repair.

All this, coupled with a head of tousled, tangled red hair and a face splashed with freckles made me a good subject for the taunts and jeers of the other children.

"Red! Red! Fell out of bed! Broke her head on a piece of corn bread!" was a common chant, especially by the boys.

All students were responsible for keeping the classroom tidy. We took turns at the end of the day cleaning the blackboard, dusting the erasers and passing the waste basket down each row of desks.

This chore proved to be especially embarrassing to me one afternoon.

The sole of one of my shoes had worn thin and the stitching had given way causing the sole to flap against the shoe with each step I took.

Magnifying my embarrassment was the sound of this flapping as I went up and down the aisles seemed to echo around the room. Giggles and side-ways glances only added to my humiliation.

It seemed an interminable task and I'm sure that that humiliation had a decisive impact on my psyche which accounts for the reason today that my closet holds more pairs of shoes than I can possibly wear out in one lifetime.

I'm sure we could have fared better. Our farm was no less prosperous than the others. However, the majority of the other farmers had accepted relief in the form of Government assistance and received monthly checks. Dad refused to 'go on the "dole" as a matter of self- esteem. Further, his two brothers and sister who had farms adjoining ours always seemed to need help at any given time. Either because of his gentle nature or because he was the oldest of the four, Dad seemed to feel an obligation to "loan" them what they needed sometimes to the extent of depriving his own family of our needs. Mother was highly resentful of this trait (or weakness) and was justified in her feelings, I believe.

Bits and Pieces

There was no public means to transport children to school due to the sparse population and large sprawls between neighbors so each family was responsible for seeing that their children got to school.

Dad drove the two of us and three other kids in our family car. These other children lived several miles from us but not far out of the way

Their father was a worker for the railroad and the family lived in a converted train boxcar near the tracks. They were of Mexican heritage with thick assents that made them a matter of curiosity to me.

Solomon, Lucy and Maria Luna were quiet and shy with eyes that darted away if you looked at them.

They carried their lunches in blue Jewel Lard buckets with perforated lids. They rarely spoke and when they did it was in words whispered to each other in their native language which they weren't allowed to use in the classroom or on the playground.

We all ate our lunches at our desks and when the Luna children brought out their meal it was comprised of a flat white tortilla wrapped around pieces of potato and shredded meat, probably mutton. They kept their eyes cast down to avoid the looks and snickers of the others in the classroom as they ate.

They were shunned on the playground and usually spent recess sitting huddled together next to the building-a sad price to pay for being different.

In every animal species, even the most intimidated underdog will seek out and eventually find one of its own who is more vulnerable and weak than they. I found these characteristics in the Luna children and today I'm ashamed to admit that I took an active role in contributing to their misery.

One morning when we stopped to pick them up they were gone. The box car was no longer in its place. Gone. As if they had never existed. They had been moved further up the tracks to follow the work, I suppose.

Our ride to school that day was strangely quiet.

Leora

Leora Tapley was a pretty girl with shiny, golden brown hair and pretty clothes. She was two or three years older than I but we were in the same grade and were best friends.

We drew a hopscotch court on the playground and spent each recess tossing our broken pieces of glass into the squares and hopping through the maze. If bad weather prevented our going outside, we were allowed to play a game of Jacks in a corner of the classroom.

I was permitted to spend the night with her occasionally and was warmly welcomed by her Mom and Dad.

She had several older brothers and sisters and they got along well together. There was a lot of laughter and good natured teasing when they were all at the dinner table.

I wondered what it would be like to live in a family like this. I never asked her to spend the night with me.

THE CHURCH AND THE DANCE HALL

In addition to housing class rooms the school building also served as a Community Center where various meetings took place and on some Saturday nights was converted into a dance hall.

Local self-taught musicians with their guitars, fiddles and accordions would congregate and dance the night away.

We never attended these affairs but there was much talk during recess the following school day about illicit flirtations and alcoholic drinks served from bottles concealed in brown paper bags.

Sometimes fist fights would break out which usually ended the dance and it was not uncommon to see someone with a black eye sitting piously on a back bench in church the following Sunday.

Sunday church was held in the schools largest classroom with services conducted by an itinerant preacher who had received a "direct and clear calling" from God Himself to go into a remote location such as ours and save souls.

Their sermons were long, loud and literal. The slightest infraction of God's laws, and there were many, was enough to send one straight to Hell and its eternal fire.

Following the sermon the congregation stood and sang a few songs from the old, worn hymnals. The preacher, sometimes tearfully, then beseeched his wayward flock to come forward and "give your life to Christ." A long prayer of dismissal followed and by mid-afternoon we were finally released.

Each Sunday a different family was expected to invite the preacher to their house for the Sunday meal which he never refused. These men, whether young or old, had appetites that would match that of a field hand.

When it was our turn to feed one, Mother would kill and fry up a couple of chickens and bake a large pan of biscuits. That along with a can or two of vegetables taken from our meager grocery stock, a fruit cobbler, and a huge bowl of creamed gravy served as the meal.

It was the custom that we kids did not eat with grown-ups when there was company but waited until they finished then we got the leftovers.

These ravenous Men of God were given first choice and multiple servings so usually only a few pieces of dark meat and the gizzards were left for us-certainly never the "pulley bone", which we would probably have fought over anyway.

BANANAS AND BOUNCING BALLS

Other than the school, the hub of our farm community consisted of a total of six or seven buildings. Four of these buildings were of prime importance to the farmers. Three were utilized for crop storage, primarily Pinto beans, and a fourth housed a mechanical cleaning operation which cleaned the residue husk and twigs left by the farm thrasher. Then the beans were weighed and re-sacked in one hundred pound burlap bags, (tow sacks), hand sewn with heavy cotton twine and stored for future sale.

Two of the buildings were General Stores and a sixth was the headquarters of a railroad foreman who supervised the workers charged with keeping the tracks repaired.

The stores were a half mile or so apart and were in stiff competition with each other for the farmers business. The competition was serious enough that the proprietors seldom spoke to each other and when one of the two was chosen over the other to handle the U.S. mail, communication ceased entirely.

Railroad tracks ran along the south side of both these businesses but only on designated days did the train stop. Otherwise the mail was thrown from the train in large canvas bags and retrieved by the store owner/postmaster to be sorted and held until the individual farmer picked it up, sometimes weeks later.

Dad usually tried to patronize both of these merchants in some way but gave the majority of his business to the smaller one who usually offered him the best credit terms. Here he was allowed to buy groceries and supplies and 'run a bill' until the fall crop had been harvested at which time the account would be settled and available for credit the next year. This "settling up" time was special for we kids as the owner would go to the candy case and fill a small brown paper bag with a mixed assortment of candy that was not available to us during the year. Free!

It was seldom necessary to buy our meat as we raised and butchered our own, but when we did it was always ten pounds of salt pork which sold for ten cents a pound. A ten dollar purchase would usually get us a few canned goods with the ARGO label, Mother's Oats which were packed in big rectangular boxes and contained a piece of dinnerware. Sometimes we purchased a can of Ovaltine with a picture of Little Orphan Annie on it. I didn't really care for either Annie or the drink.

From time to time we bought cornmeal in cloth bags with the name of the mill printed on it. Flour came in fifty pound bags made from cloth also but in a colored fabric of small printed designs. Three such matched purchases could and were often used to make a dress or boys shirt to be worn to school.

Other items such as coffee and dried fruits were sold by the pound and weighed on a scale using round metal discs, each having different weight values for balance. We usually bought these at the larger store.

The proprietors of this store were a well dressed, attractive, but rather aloof couple. Bill and Bertha Baird didn't seem to be interested in establishing anything other than a business type of relationship with their customers and their daughter, Jean, was not allowed to mingle with us when we were in the store. It was rumored that Bertha was not above bestowing her favors on some of the young farmers and hired help and Dad would be given the third degree when he returned home if he went to the store alone. He staunchly defended his innocence and I knew he was.

I committed my first and only act of thievery in this store.

I had always been fascinated by the huge stalk of bananas that hung from a large hook at the end of a rope suspended from the rafters. The bananas were shipped in while still green and slowly ripened in the dimly lit area at the rear of the store.

The aroma of these mysterious looking fruits was overwhelming and one day when everyone was busy in the front, I stole to the back of the store and gave way to temptation. I quickly snatched the banana nearest my reach and pushed it under my sweater. Terrified of being caught, I found my way out the back door and outside. With my face to the building I peeled the banana and began stuffing my mouth with large bites hardly taking time to chew.

Having successfully completed my crime, I hastily covered the green peel in the dry dirt and with knees trembling made my way to the front of the store where Dad was putting the last sack of groceries in the car.

I climbed into the back seat, pressed my face against the side window and waited for fire to rain down from heaven.

I didn't have to wait long. Half way home I was gripped with stomach cramps that were so severe I drew my knees up under my chin in an attempt to stop the pain. But to no avail. This agony continued even after we got home and I could no longer hide my misery.

Only after being administered a double dose of vile tasting Castor Oil did my digestive system unlock and I found relief-at least from my physical discomfort.

It was a child's lesson well learned that God's punishment for our transgressions can indeed be swift and severe even when dealing with a hungry five year old.

We always stopped to pick up our mail when we bought our groceries. This combination store and post office was in a smaller building than the other store. It was constructed from wood whereas the other was either brick or block.

A long high porch ran along the entire front of the building and was covered by a metal roof. Three or four stair steps leading up to the store were at each end of the porch.

Two tall gas pumps stood in front of the porch where we bought our fuel.

The proprietor was a stocky, friendly man who was a close friend of Dads and they enjoyed exchanging views on politics, weather, crops and the state of the country in general.

His wife, a plump, nervous woman with tightly permed hair and transparent skin did not mirror his disposition. She always seemed to be too warm, too tired, or too busy to be very pleasant. She wore sheer lacy or eyelet dresses always the same style but definitely from a department store or ordered from a catalogue out of our price range.

They had one daughter, Delma, who was a spoiled miniature of her mother. She was chubby and short, always wore a pretty dress and matching shoes. She had dark hair permed in tight curls and dark eyes.

They lived in rooms attached and behind the store. From a particular location from inside the store one could get a view of their living room. It was very well furnished but as cheerless and uninviting as the two females. The shades were perpetually drawn to keep out the afternoon sun and, I suppose, the curious looks of anyone who might be outside.

In spite of having absolutely nothing but their age in common, Delma and Leola became fast friends. Even to the point that she would invite Leola into the house to play while the folks took care of business.

On one occasion I was asked and allowed to enter this mysterious realm with them and was astonished by my surroundings.

All the rooms were semi-dark with the shades drawn. The furniture in the living room was perfectly arranged but shrouded with covers. The kitchen and dining room shared the same space and had gleaming white appliances. Two other rooms with their doors closed were bedrooms I was told. But the most impressive room was a play room lined with shelves holding every conceivable toy a child could imagine.

Shirley Temple and Effanbee dolls with real hair and glass eyes that opened and closed sat primly on the top shelves obviously never touched or played with; a musical Jack-in-the Box that played Pop-Goes-The-Weasel; books, blocks, a red white and blue jump rope with wooden handles and a child size table and chairs were just a few of the things here. If it was to be had, it was owned by this little girl.

I became fascinated by a brightly colored ball in the corner.

Seeing my interest, Delma was quick to remind me that no one was allowed to play with it because it was "magic" and if you bounced it, it would go so high it would disappear into the sky.

We soon heard Dad calling that he was ready to leave and when we came out into the light of the store, I'm sure I had a look of sheer wonderment on my face.

One little girl with so much. Three little girls with so little. I made up my mind that day that I would become a store owner when I grew up.

It would be some time before we made another trip to the store. We had enough groceries to sustain us for another month or so but the image of all that "luxury" stayed in my mind for days. Back in my world I took inventory of my toys. One doll with painted hair and eyes. Mother had sewn it a dress and matching bloomers from a worn out dress of her own. The scrap of an old quilt was her blanket and I dearly loved this doll.

Our jump rope was of rough hemp and Dad had tied a knot in each end to prevent it from raveling. By tying one end to a post and one of us turning it in high arches holding the free end, we took turns 'running in' and jumping until we missed, thereby allowing the other a turn. No Jack-in-the-Box or blocks, but we had our books and old Sears and Montgomery Ward catalogues from which we cut our paper dolls. These things were familiar and comfortable and touchable.

A few months went by and some need prompted us to go back to the store.

My folks and sisters walked ahead of me as we entered the store. For some unknown reason I lagged behind and lingered on the steps. I glanced down and there was the Magic Ball!

Curious to see if it really would disappear, I picked it up and slammed it against the porch floor. To my horror I watched it bounce straight up and slam into the unprotected overhead light fixture.

The sound of shattering glass caught the immediate attention of my Dad and the store owner's wife, Nellie.

Two sets of angry eyes welded me to the spot.

Wringing her hands and dabbing at her damp forehead with a dainty handkerchief that had been nesting in the cleavage of her ample bosom, she wailed about the cost of replacing the bulb and fixture.

Long accustomed to female emotional outbursts, Dad calmly told me to find the broom and when I finished sweeping up my mess to go sit in the car. His voice was calm but held an unspoken promise that more was forthcoming at a less public time and place.

Not a word was spoken by any of us on the return trip.

It was a long ride home.

After sundown, I lit the kerosene lamp on the kitchen table (my chore) and sat down to wait for Dad to finish the milking and learn of my fate.

Suddenly Mother rushed into the house, grabbed me by the arm and pulled me roughly outside. She waved her hand eastward and pointed in the direction of the General Store. Even from this distance ugly orange flames could be seen licking at the sky.

"Now see what you did?" She shrieked. "You broke that light!" "Now the store is on fire!" "Where will we get our groceries?"

She shoved me aside and rushed toward the barn in search of Dad, leaving me terrified and alone in the dark.

Whether or not she actually believed that a broken light bulb could cause an electrical malfunction so severe that it could have such disastrous results, I'll never know. But the belief that my recklessness had caused the merchant to lose his means of livelihood and ultimately bring starvation to my entire family was so overwhelming that I became physically ill.

As if by some strange premonition of trouble, Mother Cat was waiting for me under the kitchen table. I hugged her tightly in my arms and prayed fervently that God would somehow reveal his mercy by providing for both the store owner and my family and if possible, spare me the agonies if hell which I was sure had now become my ultimate fate.

Weeks later the word was out that the fire was not at the store and had been an act of arson.

A neighboring farmer had rented a space in the Co-op warehouse to store his previous harvest.

A failed spring crop coupled with the untimely death of his overworked wife had depleted his meager income and the desperate man had torched the building in the hope of collecting a few dollars form the insurance company.

Interestingly, before this news was revealed, Dad still had not as much as reprimanded me for the ruckus I had caused. He was wise enough to know that my tormented conscience had rendered a far greater punishment than he could administer.

Even so, I received no indication from either my Mother or my God that I was off the hook, lest at some time in the future I should again succumb to the sin of being a child, I suppose.

SIMPLY CHRISTMAS

Compared to today's extravagance of overspending, overeating, giving to get, and measuring the worth of a gift by the cost of the purchase, our Christmases would probably have been viewed as being impoverished. But in reality they were—Christmas.

Our school rooms were decorated with paper chains made from strips of red and green construction paper with each link secured by using the white paste from the big jars.

Each class presented a program and every child had a role in the play. The theme of the skit was always based on the birth of Jesus and the audience, which was made up of our parents joined with us in singing "Away In A Manger", " Silent Night", Oh Little Town of Bethlehem" and all the other familiar Christmas Carols.

Today's ACLU would surely take to the streets in protest. Fortunately, neither the ACLU nor streets were in existence in our small world at that time.

My parents never told us there was a Santa Clause. It just didn't seem to be in keeping with Dad's no nonsense way of teaching us to deal with the realities of life. But at the end of the program a portly man in a red Santa suit and fake white beard climbed on the stage and began handing out cellophane bags of hard candies to each child. My sisters and I may have been the only children there who were not deceived by this disguise. We knew this Santa was really a bachelor named Jack Williams, the only man in the county who apparently had more than enough to eat and thereby able to fill out the oversized red suit.

Our Christmases at home were also meager by today's comparison but evoked the same pre-Christmas excitement as children feel today, I'm sure.

We seldom had a tree. Our tiny house would hardly accommodate one, but we laid out our stockings the night before and found it difficult to sleep. Eventually, we would hear Dad stirring around lighting the fire and at daylight we could get up.

Emptying the stockings was a real treat. There was an orange or apple, some nuts of various kinds and a piece or two of hard candy. Usually the family shared a box of chocolate covered cherries which were rationed out day to day.

We each received one gift and the success of the fall crop had a direct bearing on the type of gift. One Christmas in particular I received an new dress for my doll which Mother had made and hand sewn from scraps left over from a dress she had made for me. There were matching bloomers and best of all a tiny pair of moccasins made from the fleece lining of Dad's worn out overcoat.

A more prosperous year provided for store bought gifts. These were wrapped in bright tissue paper printed with green leaves and holly berries.

We took turns opening our gifts. Nadine received a beautiful China Victorian doll. Her dress was painted a brilliant royal blue. Her long golden curls were pulled back from her Cameo type face with a jeweled bow and even the nails on her tiny hands were painted a bright pink. This was a beautiful piece of Dresden but far too fragile to withstand a subsequent tantrum perpetrated by her owner.

Leola's gift was a baby doll with a rubber face, arms and legs. The body was of soft cloth and she was dressed in cuddly pink pajamas with a matching blanket.

I unwrapped my gift. It was a little green tractor with thick, black rubber tires. I sensed Dad watching me closely and struggled but couldn't conceal my disappointment.

Reliving that Christmas today, I realize with considerable regret that by allowing my childish jealousy of my sisters pretty dolls to prevail, I failed to grasp the significance of the sentiment associated with this gift from my father of a little toy John Deere Tractor.

If there was not enough money for individual gifts, there was always at least one for us to share as a family. Once it was a game of Chinese checkers, another time a set of Dominos. Dad taught us how to play Dominos and a bidding game called Forty-Two, the rudiments of which have now escaped my memory.

Mother would roast a hen which had been fattened up for just this occasion. This and a large pan of cornbread dressing and giblet gravy made a wonderful meal and great leftovers.

This was a good day at our house. The kitchen was warm and smelled of sage dressing and homemade bread. There was virtually no bickering or arguing and we stayed up later than usual to enjoy this time.

HARD WORK AND A HEADACHE

Dad began preparing the land for spring planting as soon as the ground thawed after the winter snows had melted.

One of the neighbor farmers owned a blacksmith forge where he would take the plows for sharpening. He occasionally took me with him and I would turn the heavy iron handle of the forge to keep the coal embers hot. He would hold the tips of the plows in these embers until they turned red from the heat then with heavy tongs he would remove them and place them on an anvil where he would hammer them with a heavy sledge hammer until they were sharp. Our faces would be covered with soot and the smell of the smoke was pungent and lingered in our nostrils hours later. With the exception of the pride I felt that I was being helpful, I could have forgone this job.

Spring planting usually began in mid or late April and was completed by the first part of May. We planted Pinto beans, corn and a small amount of sugar cane for cattle feed. Late in the summer the crops would be cultivated to reduce weed growth. This was done using small cultivator plows hitched to the tractor but more productively by hand using a hoe.

We worked in the fields, going out early in the morning before the heat of the day. At high noon we took a break for dinner which usually consisted of the previous night's leftovers. We rested for half an hour or so then went back to the field and worked until after the sun went down. But this was not the end of our day as there were still chores to be done.

Nadine and Mother cooked supper while Dad and I did the outside chores. He had taught me to milk a cow when I was four or five years old. He had assigned me a gentle old Jersey cow named Beauty that I close to consider a pet. Mother Cat followed me into the stall and I learned to aim a stream of milk in her direction which usually hit its mark somewhere on her face and she would lick it off her whiskers.

The pigs and chickens were fed, eggs gathered, and Dad chopped the wood for the stove. We filled the lamps with coal oil and then we could sit down to eat.

Nadine and I were to take turns washing the supper dishes and I cannot remember one instance when an argument didn't erupt regarding whose turn it was. Dad finally marked a calendar by switching our initials to every other day but we still found reason to quarrel about this chore.

A tired, dirty crew fell into bed each evening to awaken long before sun-up the next day to begin the process over again.

There was very little time for play or recreation but on rainy days we stayed inside and played with our paper dolls. We made houses out of cardboard boxes and cut their furniture out of the pages from a wall paper catalogue but again, as seemed to be our inevitable lot, we usually ended up arguing over one thing or another and were made to put our paper dolls away until we "could learn to get along together." This was a challenge neither seemed to be up to. The next time I went to play with them I discovered all their heads had been torn off. Nadine gleefully took the credit but when I complained, Dad wearily repeated his chorus of "Keep your things out of her way."

There seemed to be no referee or mediator to intervene in our petty, childish bickering. Dad spent the majority of his time outdoors and Mother was simply a third party in our quarreling. Inevitably, she would slam out of the house exclaiming that she was going back 'home' where she would "never have to put up with you damned kids again!" I spent anxious hours dreading what it would be like to live in a house without a Mother in it.

As we grew older our quarreling grew more and more bitter and physical. Nadine was larger and stronger than I and her attacks often left me physically hurt. Once she twisted my arm behind my back with such force that my shoulder was sprained and I was unable to put my arm in the sleeve of my dress for several weeks. Another time she tripped me as I walked in front of the stove causing me to fall and gash my head on the hearth. Even though Dad was there to witness this, he simply told Mother to put a wet cloth on my head and left the house. As with all head wounds there seemed to be a profuse amount of blood which eventually dried and mated in my hair. This wound left a scar on my head which even today requires some rather skillful coiffing to conceal.

I eventually learned to keep the minor injuries to myself, but in all the sixteen years of life I spent with my family, I was never able to completely escape these encounters with my older sister. Unlike Dorothy and Toto who did eventually arrive at the Emerald City, I seemed always to be just shy of reaching "Out-Of-Their-Way".

Our summers were long, unpleasant intervals in our dysfunctional lives and I looked forward to fall and returning to school where for at least a portion of each day there was harmony and warm companionship.

Fall also meant that new people came into our lives, though only temporarily.

There was a limited amount of time in which to harvest the bean crop before the fall rains began. The beans were cut and left on the ground in their rows. Hired workers would follow along behind the tractor with pitchforks and pile the beans in small mounds spaced a foot or two apart. Later these mounds would be loaded onto a wagon, hauled to the end of the row and thrashed mechanically with the beans separated from the hulls. The beans would then be sacked in one hundred pound burlap bags which were hand sewn closed with heavy cotton twine and at last they were ready to be taken to a warehouse for cleaning.

At the start of harvest Dad would drive to a town about fifty miles away where there was a train station. Young men who had hitched a ride on a freight train and been ordered off when the train stopped were eager to find work. Dad would hire four or five of these men and bring them home.

They were given room and board and paid a dollar a day plus their Bull Durham or Prince Albert tobacco. They were housed on cots in the half dug-out. They carried their belongings in a bed roll and sometimes had a guitar and harmonica or fiddle.

With the help of a neighbor's wife, Mother spent all day cooking meals for these men. Breakfast consisted of fried ham or salt pork, huge pans of biscuits, 'red-eye' or creamed gravy and pots of coffee. The noon meal was usually Pinto beans, some type of meat, cornbread, and if the ingredients were available, a fruit cobbler. Supper was a duplicate of the noon meal with extra bread or gravy if none was left from the previous meal.

The food was cooked on a wood burning stove. Our little house was always hot and with the seemingly endless work she had to do, it's no wonder that our mother could be so difficult sometimes.

After the evening meal, the Harvest Hands as they were referred to, sat outside the dug-out and played their musical instruments, sometimes singing and yodeling. I would occasionally sit on our porch step and listen to their songs and muted voices as they talked and joked with each other.

The smell of smoke from their hand rolled cigarettes would filter into the evening air and I wondered where the mysterious men came from and where they would go when their work for us was finished.

These young men were not mere drifters. They were on the road to earn the only living that was available at the time and they sent most of their wages home. Others were employed through a government agency known as the Civilian Conservation Corps (CCC). Men between the ages of eighteen and twenty-five planted trees, built parks, worked on flood control projects and other work that helped conserve the environment. They were housed in army type barracks or tents and received thirty dollars a month, twenty-two of which was sent home to their dependents. Between 1933 and 1941 over 3,000,000 men served in the C.C.C.

The men that worked the farms were not part of this government effort but definitely a part of the otherwise jobless population prevalent at the time. They worked until the harvest was done then with their bed rolls and musical instruments, Dad drove them back to the train station and they continued their life on the road.

One day in late fall, an older man appeared on our farm. He was a stocky built man with baggy clothes, a big straw hat and had a handlebar moustache.

He carried a small, worn satchel of belongings. He was tired, hungry and looking for work.

The fall work was finished for the most part but Dad took him in, offered him a small salary and he stayed on our place for several months. He had a soft Spanish accent and a low, gentle voice. Dad let him sleep on a cot in the kitchen and he helped with the daily chores.

Normally, I was not allowed to mingle with the Hired Hands but Dad trusted this man and although I was shy around him, Vicente, Mother Cat and I formed an odd companionship.

He helped with the milking, always pouring a small amount in a jar lid for

Mother Cat. He chopped the wood for our kitchen stove while I waited nearby to carry it in. We sat on overturned galvanized buckets and he taught me to shell corn for the chickens.

I have no recollection of having a real conversation with him but felt a bonding of spirit with Vicente and became strangely melancholy when, one day in late Spring, after a quiet conversation with Dad they shook hands, and carrying the old, worn satchel in one hand and a gnarled wooden walking stick he had come to rely on to steady his uneven gate in the other, he walked slowly away without a glance in my direction.

I watched until his image became a small dot against the horizon. As near as I could tell he never once looked back. As quietly as he had entered into our lives, he had exited it—but to where?

CIGARS AN GUNS

Shortly after breakfast one morning in 1935 a big black Pickup truck drove up along the side of our barn and two men got out. Both of them were dressed in dark khaki clothes and were smoking big brown cigars.

Dad seemed to be expecting them and after hastily instructing Mother to "keep the girls inside", he went out to meet them. Leola was still an infant and asleep but Mother rushed to the window and naturally, Nadine and I followed.

Dad met the two men and the three of them stood talking, occasionally striding over to the corral where our cows had been pinned up for the night. One of the men walked back to their truck and took out a gun with a long barrel.

Panicked, I asked, "What is he going to do?"

"They are going to kill our cows." Mother's voice had a trace of hysteria that bordered on my own feelings and I stared at her in disbelief.

"Why?' I was crying now. "All of them?"

"Probably, I don't know." She answered my questions in reverse.

I was stricken with terror and disbelief and more questions.

Why?

Not Ole' Beauty!

Why would Dad let this happen?

Before I could verbalize these concerns, I heard four rapid gun shots-then silence.

I had faced away from the window but turned back now in time to see the two men climb back into their truck and drive away.

Four of our cows lay on the ground and the rest were running nervously around the corral yard amid the dust raised by their hoofs.

Unable to restrain my fear and concern for Ole Beauty, I pushed past Mother and Nadine and ran out the door.

The smell of gun and cigar smoke still lingered in the air as I raced barefoot, with legs trembling to the stall that had been assigned to my cow.

And there she was, contentedly chewing her cud, blissfully unaware that four of her barnyard companions had just taken a bullet squarely between the eyes and were even now being loaded onto a sled hitched to the tractor.

I had asked Dad about this sled while I watched him hammer it together a few weeks earlier and his response had simply been, "We're going to need it."

It was years later, in high school civics class before my question was answered.

A federal agency had been formed for just this purpose. Known as the Drought Relief Service, the government paid farmers fourteen to twenty dollars a head for their cattle. This was considered to be a better price than could be obtained at market. Fifty percent of these cows were destroyed and the remainder given to the Federal Surplus Relief Corps to be used for food distribution. It was a necessary and noble cause to survive the Depression, I suppose, but to this day, subconsciously, I'm a little suspicious of powerful government officials and if they smoke cigars my distrust is further compounded.

THE PLAY HOUSE

We returned to the routine of daily chores and school.

Nadine and I contracted the usual childhood diseases of Chicken Pox and Mumps. The following spring we were exposed to Measles and Whooping Cough and were unfortunate enough to be afflicted with them combined together.

In retrospect, it's a wonder that children in that era survived their childhood and many didn't. Treatment was only as good as the home remedies that applied to the ailment and were mostly ineffective. Vicks Rub, a few drops of coal oil or turpentine in a spoon of sugar followed by a flannel cloth worn on the chest was the most common treatment and as far as I know did little other than cause a rash to pop out on your chest which lasted well into the year.

We suffered through bouts of delirium brought on by raging fevers, coughed until we were blue in the face and reeked of Vicks.

We both missed a considerable amount of school but again Dad took up the slack and tutored us. Altogether it was a miserable time for us all but eventually we improved. Unfortunately my lung capacity was compromised and that coupled with cigarette smoking during my college years created a health problem that I contend with even today, years later.

We returned to school late in the year, successfully completed our grades and resumed our routines at home.

That summer Dad gave us permission to have playhouses in the rock house and dug-out since neither was in use. Nadine got first choice of the two and I considered myself lucky when, true to her nature, she chose the larger dug-out.

We set up housekeeping with our dolls, empty tin cans, wooden boxes for tables and overturned buckets for chairs.

Nadine came to my house as 'Mrs. Smith' and invited me to visit her a little later.

I hesitated at the door reluctant to walk in reacting to my dread of this place. "Come in." I heard her voice call from inside.

As I walked through the door I glanced around to where I thought she might be and barley missed being crushed as she sprang down from the ledge above the door. To my surprise, and hers, as she jumped she scraped her head on the rafter above the ledge and pulled back a small piece of flesh on her forehead.

As she lay stunned on the ground I couldn't help but feel some satisfaction for her misery. Ah! Sweet revenge! And I hadn't had to lift a finger.

But my pleasure was short lived. She jumped to her feet and ran outside. Her piercing screams brought both Dad and Mother on the run. She fell to the ground, sobbing hysterically, clasping her head with one hand and pointing at me with the other.

Mother quickly scooped her up and rushed into the house to attend to the scrape.

My heart sank as I saw Dad removing his belt and striding angrily toward me. I felt his tight grip on my arm and the belt slash against my bare legs.

No inquiry. No trial. No jury. But two unjust judges had presumed me guilty and this punishment was my dues.

Not surprisingly, Nadine's sobs ceased with the first strike of the belt.

Humiliated and hurting, but determined not to cry, I stood with my feet planted firmly on the spot until my whipping was over then walked slowly and painfully toward the barn where I found Mother Cat dozing in her favorite spot in the sun and gathered her up in my arms. I buried my face in her soft fur and whispered tearfully, "Someday, Mother Cat. Someday".

This was not my first experience of being on the blistering end of Dad's belt nor would it be the last. He rarely resorted to such extreme methods of punishment and when he did he usually administered it more fairly. Surely on this day he was overcome by the frustration of our continual squabbling. But I believe that incident spawned my resolve to find a way when I grew up to leave and never again return to this unhappy place.

FIRST LOVE

Fall arrived nudging the long, hot, quarrelsome days of summer in to the background and we returned to school.

I was in the sixth grade, had a new teacher and fell in love.

If there was a Brad Pitt in the thirties, it was C. W. Bourne, the teacher's son. He had large round brown eyes and sun streaked blond hair. He didn't wear the bib overalls like the farm boys wore but instead dressed in corduroy pants and white shirts and nice looking shoes.

We spent recesses walking around the playground together ignoring the giggles and teasing of the other kids as we passed by them.

Sometimes we sat on the school house steps discussing what we planned to be when we grew up. In the classroom we engaged in good-natured competition as to which one could get the best grades and usually ended in a tie.

As we sat on the steps one day, C.W. reached into his pocket and pulled out a ring. It had an adjustable silver colored band and a stone of multi-colored glass. He held it in the open palm of his hand and told me he wanted me to "be his girl" even through the summer after school was out.

No doubt this ring was a prize from his most recent purchase of a box of Cracker Jacks, but I saw it as an equal to the Hope Diamond even after it began to turn my finger green a few weeks later.

I wore the ring home and shyly but proudly showed it off to Dad. He glanced at it briefly then in a voice that I had come to recognize as meaning serious business said, "You're never going to amount to anything if you spend the time in which you should be studying chasing boys."

Chasing boys?

From across the room I saw Nadine listening and watching with narrowed eyes.

How I treasured this ring. It was my first piece of jewelry and I wore it with pride and perhaps no small degree of smugness.

No jewel was ever cared for with such diligence. In the evenings I removed it and placed it in a safe place on a shelf above the wash basin stand. I certainly didn't want to take a chance of losing it as I went about my chores. Otherwise, I wore it constantly.

One evening during supper, Nadine tapped me on the hand and asked" Where is your precious ring?"

Realizing I had forgotten to put it on again after chores, I jumped up from the table to retrieve it from the shelf.

There was the ring. The band was twisted and broken. The glass stone was crushed in the mounting.

I cried out in shock and surprise. How could she do this? What was I going to tell C.W.?

I showed the ring to Dad. "That ring was a lot of nonsense." He said. "Eat your supper."

I slept very little that night, grieving over the ruined ring and dreading to tell C.W. what had happened. Resentment and hatred for this demon possessed sister sleeping peacefully beside me gnawed at my soul.

The first recess bell rang too soon, and as we walked around the playground together, I began to explain about the ring. C.W. stopped and looked at me for a long moment then turned and ran back inside the school house.

This was the end of our romance. C.W. never spoke to me again. Occasionally I would catch him glancing at me in the classroom but he quickly turned away when I looked in his direction. He rejoined the other boys in their games at recess and went out of his way to avoid me.

There is no love like first 'puppy love' and no ache compared to the first broken heart. I was sure that I was doomed to suffer forever.

To an eight year old 'forever' recovery time takes a lifetime of about three or four months.

TOUGH AS A RABBIT

I never spent much time alone with Dad. The other girls didn't seem to have the problem, but I always felt awkward and insignificant when we were together. He did take me along with him occasionally but the time usually passed with little conversation. Still, I treasured these times because, always the teacher, there was usually a lesson to learn.

In the spring of 1938 there was a surge in the jack rabbit population and they were destroying the young crops that were beginning to sprout.

One morning after breakfast, Dad said to me, "Get your coat on. Let's get rid of some of these pests."

He reached for the shot gun which he kept high on a rack over the kitchen door and we set off on our mission.

We walked through the pasture east of the house for some distance before we spotted our first unfortunate prey.

A large jack rabbit jumped from behind a sage bush and with kangaroo leaps bounded ahead of us, his long hind legs thumping against the ground as he bounced away.

I covered my ears as Dad raised the gun, put the rabbit in its sights and fired. The impact caused the animal to leap slightly in the air then tumble to the ground. I hated this, but I didn't dare let on lest Dad would decide against taking me again.

As we approached where the rabbit lay, he suddenly sprang to his feet and with great bounds was off into the distance again having only been temporarily stunned by the discharge of buckshot hitting the dirt near him.

In my excitement to see that Dad's shot had missed its mark, I pretended not to hear the mild oath he muttered under his breath as we watched the rabbit's long ears disappear over the ridge.

"Wow!" "That was a tough rabbit!" I exclaimed.

Dad looked down at me for a long moment. Then he knelt down on one knee and I felt him grip my arms through my thin coat.

"We all have to be tough." He said. "You remember this. There will be times in your life when you think the situation you are in is too much to bear; that the pain will never end and you might as well give up. When trouble comes, tell yourself that you can make it one more hour, one more day, one more week. Every time you get knocked down, make yourself get back up again. Surely, you can be as tough as that rabbit."

I had no way of knowing then how many times I would need to rely on that wisdom as I journeyed through life.

A BABY AND A PROBLEM

Late one night in mid-December Dad shook us awake and told us to get dressed. He helped us struggle sleepily into our clothes and hurried us out into the cold night to the car.

Bewildered and groggy, I wondered where we were going and why Mother had stayed behind in bed.

"You are spending the night with your cousin," was the brief explanation he offered as we drove through the darkness toward his brother's house.

I adored this cousin. She had pretty clothes, a room of her own and pretty things. Almost always she had a new package of Double mint Gum and sometimes she would break a stick in half and share it with us.

She was several years older than I and I looked upon her as sort of an idol. Nevertheless, visiting at this late hour was odd but I resisted asking questions as Dad seemed pre-occupied and apprehensive.

We pulled into the yard of their darkened house and Dad hurried up the porch steps and knocked loudly on the door, leaving us in the car. Uncle Lester came to the door holding a kerosene lamp. He and Dad exchanged a few hastily spoken words and he went back inside and I could see more lamps were being lit.

Dad returned to the car and told us to get out. Leola had fallen asleep again so he lifted her from the back seat and carried her up the steps with Nadine striding along beside him and me tagging sleepily behind.

Aunt Rhoda and Bonnie Rae met us at the door. Aunt had her coat on and followed Dad outside and got in the car. Bonnie Rae herded us into her bedroom where she put Leola, still sleeping, under the covers of her bed.

She then turned to Nadine and me and asked, "What do you think is happening?" She was smiling so I sensed that whatever it was, it must be something nice and felt a little less anxious. But as I heard the car speed away my uneasiness returned.

"I know what's happening." Nadine boasted. "But she doesn't," nodding her head toward me. "She doesn't need to know."

Ignoring this spiteful remark directed at me, Bonnie Rae asked, "Would you rather get a brother or another sister?"

Suddenly the dawn broke. We were getting another baby!

"Doesn't matter to me." Nadine shrugged.

Another baby.

Another sister?

Still wearing our clothes, we bedded down on pallets on the floor next to our cousins bed.

I tossed restlessly most of the night. I hoped Dad would pick us up early tomorrow.

Morning finally came. We sat down to eat breakfast but I didn't feel hungry. I ate a few bites then went to sit near the front door to wait for the sound of our car driving into the yard.

It was mid-afternoon. A long night with little sleep had taken its toll and soon I abandoned my post by the door in exchange for a more comfortable spot on the couch.

I was aroused by Dad's voice urging me to wake up. "It's time to go. He said. "You've got a baby brother at home."

A brother! I jumped hurriedly to my feet and grabbed my coat. This time I was the one rushing to keep up with Dad while Nadine lagged behind.

Mother was still in bed with the new baby nestled in the curve of one arm. Nadine pushed ahead and stood looking down at both of them for what seemed a long time and then without a word, turned and left the room.

"What's his name?" I wanted to know.

"Well he'll be named after your daddy," Mother said. "But you can call him Junior."

Now no boy wants to be permanently saddled to the moniker 'Junior' and soon after he started first grade he informed us that he would no longer answer to that name and instead wanted to be known by his initials, A.T. But Junior seemed to be branded on my brain and unless his peers are around or I make a conscious effort not to, I still refer to him by that name even though he is in his late sixties, and he is gracious enough to let me get away with it.

It was several weeks before Mother was back on her feet. She was in her mid-thirties and physically run down and Junior had been born several weeks premature. As with the rest of us, with the exception of Nadine, he was delivered by my dad, assisted by a female relative or our neighbor, Mrs. Morris.

She was a plump, grandmotherly woman with silver white hair and talked incessantly. She and her husband, Tom, had raised a family of three sons and two daughters. Most of them were grown adults now. The entire family helped us during harvest time and lived in a half dug-out a few miles from us.

She came each day to help out and sometimes, while she cooked our supper, she would let me hold the baby near the warmth of the stove.

Now it was the days at school that seemed long and for the first time since I can remember, I looked forward to getting home.

We didn't have a rocking chair but I would sit holding him in my arms and rock slowly back and forth until he fell asleep then Mrs. Morris would take him and put him back in bed with Mother.

By the end of December the winter had turned severe. It was bitterly cold. Snow swept through the area and banked deep drifts against the house and barn.

Using the tractor, Dad was able to keep the road fairly passable but the continual falling snow caused us to stay out of school for several weeks. Again Dad resumed tutoring us at home.

Very early one morning in January we were awakened by the folks telling us to get up and get dressed. Something was wrong with our baby. His breathing was shallow and his coloring was a strange shade of grey.

Dad was hastily putting quilts in the back seat of the car and telling us to get our coats on and get into the car. We had to get to a doctor.

They wrapped Junior in warm blankets. We piled into the car and Dad pulled out onto the heavily snow covered road in route to town forty-five miles away.

Periodically, he would stop the car and take the baby from Mother and place a handkerchief over his mouth. He would then gently breathe into his mouth until his color improved and then he drove on.

We arrived in town around daybreak. The doctor's residence adjoined his office and Dad knocked loudly at his door.

The old country doctor was the only one in the county. His practice covered treating everything from diarrhea to snake bites and he was accustomed to being routed out of bed at all hours of the night any day of the week. It was not un-common that compensation for his services amounted to a few dozen eggs or a cured ham.

Lights went on inside the office. Dad returned to the car and he and Mother carried Junior inside while we girls waited in the car.

Inside, the doctor noticed Junior's color and quickly checked his respiratory responses with his cold stethoscope and was alarmed to discover that one lung was not functioning at all. He advised the folks that Junior's survival depended on getting him treated with oxygen and the only hospital equipped with this type of service was almost a hundred miles away and through a narrow, mountainous canyon.

Our car did not have a heater and the doctor quickly arranged for the town pharmacist, Mr. Dodds, whose car was equipped with one, to drive us to the hospital.

We transferred over to the other car and were on our way.

Snow was falling heavily as we turned off the narrow country street and onto the two lane highway and began the arduous drive through the long mountain pass. More and more frequently it was necessary for Dad to assist Junior with his breathing.

The heater warmed the car but I felt a chill that had nothing to do with the weather. Mother was clearly agitated and Dad, whom we always looked to for assurance, was fully occupied with caring for Junior.

I don't recall words being spoken between any of us on the seemingly endless ride. The only sound was that of the windshield wipers as they labored to clear the thick, wet snow piling up on the windshield.

It was early evening when we finally pulled into the emergency entrance to the hospital. We hastily exited the car and Dad rushed in carrying Junior to the admission desk. We were given immediate attention. The Charge Nurse noticed Mother's exhausted state and recommended that she be hospitalized also.

Left alone in the huge waiting room while Mother and Junior were being tended to, we three girls must have looked like scraggly waifs as we sat huddled together on the large couch. We had never seen a hospital before let alone been inside of one and the vastness of the lobby coupled with the stressful circumstance of being there was intimidating. Even Nadine was subdued.

We were startled when a slim Nun in a white habit suddenly appeared and sat down in the chair across from us.

"How long has it been since you children have had anything to eat?" Her voice was low and soft.

We looked at each other shyly. We hadn't thought of food since leaving home-how long ago?

Characteristically bold, Nadine spoke up. "There wasn't time-".

Again, "Follow me."

She motioned as she rose and started walking across the polished floor.

We trailed timidly behind her as she glided down the corridor. The only sounds were that of our footsteps and the rustle of her long starched skirts.

She pushed a heavy door open and we stepped into the sterile brightly lit kitchen of the hospital. It was a huge room with stainless steel cabinets and table-tops. The floor was covered with large black and white square tiles. As with the rest of the hospital, there was a pungent odor of disinfectant.

She waved us to a table and almost before we were seated, she had given us each a half dozen soda crackers and a tall glass if cold milk. We ate hungrily and when we were finished she brushed up the crumbs, put our empty glasses in the sink and again we found ourselves following her down the hallway.

This time she took us into another section of the hospital where nurses were rushing from room to room. Their shoes squeaked slightly as they hurried across the polished floor. She signaled for us to keep quiet and opened a door to a small, white room and let us have a quick look at Junior. He was in a high bed covered by an oxygen tent. His lips and cheeks were pink again and he was sleeping peacefully. From there we took another hallway to the room where Mother was. She was still very agitated and tearful. Dad was reassuring her that things would be alright and he would soon be back to take them both home.

We said our lingering goodbyes and the nurse escorted us back to the main lobby.

As we stepped into the frigid night air we could see the white exhaust from the pipe of the car.

Who knows how long he had waited, but Mr. Dodds had the car warming up and we climbed wearily inside for the long ride back home.

Leola was prone to having earaches and probably as a result of our on and off exposure to the cold air, she was struck with one now and began to cry. Dad bundled her in one of the blankets and held her on his lap in the front seat..

Nadine and I burrowed into our quilts in the back and she was soon asleep. But I was uneasy. If you were sick enough to get put in a hospital, were you sick enough to die?

What if Junior died? What if Mother died? Nadine was the oldest. Would she then be the Mother?

It was too much to reckon with. It had been a long, emotional, stressful day. The snow chains on the car beat a rhythmic clunk on the frozen surface of the road and I finally fell into a fitful sleep and dreamed of angels who wore long white robes, lived in hospitals and shared their food with hungry children.

A HOUSE WITHOUT A MOTHER

It was almost daylight when we arrived back in our town.

Mr. Dodds helped transfer us back into our car. Dad paid him for his trouble and we headed home.

The roads were still covered with snow but the ground was frozen so there was little danger of getting stuck. We took the side road to pick up Mrs. Morris who would again help us out during the day until Mother was home again.

Dad started a fire and while he took care of chores that had gone unattended outside, she prepared a breakfast of pork sausage, biscuits and gravy.

It had been almost twenty-four hours since he had slept or had a real meal and Dad looked weary and had very little to say as we ate.   Mrs. Morris insisted that we all try to get some sleep and we took her advice, stretching across our beds and fell asleep almost instantly.

As before, she came each day to help take care of us. She made sure we continued reading since we hadn't returned to school yet. She put drops of warm oil in Leola's ears to stop the ear aches and soothed her crying until she fell asleep. She helped us cut out our paper dolls and was an impartial referee settling our childish squabbles. But her biscuits didn't get dark and crusty on the bottom like Mother's did and more often than not the gravy was lumpy. Being less discriminating, Mother Cat enjoyed extra portions.

I missed my brother and Mother. Though she had often made threats of leaving and never coming back, in reality she had never spent a night away from us before.

Even a poorly designed jig-saw puzzle needs all of its pieces in order to be complete and two of our pieces were missing.

Our house took on a surreal atmosphere and I was eager for Dad to go bring them home as he had promised.

The morning he left to pick them up was clear and cold with a brisk wind blowing from the North. He had picked Mrs. Morris up earlier than usual and before he left had instructed her to keep a fire going in the stove well into the evening when he expected to be back.

He had made a last minute decision to take Nadine with him. She had been pouting and sullen since we came back and knowing how unpredictable her behavior could be, I guess his decision was a wise one. It certainly made for a far less stressful day for me as I was relieved of the necessity of trying to "stay out of her way" but I felt envious, nevertheless, that she was chosen to go.

It was well past dusk when we saw the headlights of the car in the distance. I watched through the north window until the car drove into the yard then ran to the door to greet them. Mrs. Morris pulled me back with a stern warning that opening the door would let in the cold air. "They'll get in when they get in." She admonished.

Dad carried Junior in completely wrapped in warm blankets, and Mother and Nadine followed close behind. Mrs. Morris quickly closed the door behind them and Dad began peeling the blankets away.

I was surprised to see that Junior looked as if he had grown. He was sound asleep breathing easily and normally. The doctor at the hospital had put him on a formula of canned milk   mixed with water and Karo syrup and he seemed to be thriving well. Mother looked rested too but not especially glad to be back with us.

"Well." She said. "They told me to get as much rest as I could, but I can tell by this mess," she waved her hands toward the stove, "that's not going to happen." I looked around to see what she was referring to. Mrs. Morris had kept the left over supper warming on the back of the stove and our dishes hadn't been washed yet. I made a decision that I would try to help out more and even stop arguing with Nadine about whose turn it was to do the dishes, but as with most childish, well intended decisions, of course, I slacked off within a matter of time.

Dad let me hold Junior while they ate. Afterward, he took Mrs. Morris home and we all went to bed as soon as he returned.

The weather improved enough to enable us to go back to school and our lives gradually returned to normal again.

LOSING AN OLD FRIEND

One evening as we carried our heavy buckets of milk to the house, Dad looked down at me and said as a matter-of-fact, "Ole' Beauty is in pretty bad shape. She's been a good cow, but she is old and weak and I don't think she'll be around much longer." Noticing my distress, he added, "It's not going to change things to start whining about it."

It was true that she had grown frail and weak. Her hip bones protruded like blades and her ribs were visible enough to count.

She had stopped producing milk long ago and had only escaped the government agent's bullet by dad's intervention.

I had begun to heat the water I mixed with her dry bran and in the evenings I covered her old, thin body with gunny sacks to ward off the night chill.

With childish naivety I chose to believe that with continued good care she could 'get well' so I was crushed when I found her one morning lying on her side with her legs extended from her body; her breath labored and spasmodic.

Unmindful of the dank earth in the stall, I sat down and placed her large head in my lap. I stroked her neck and ears while Mother Cat prowled nervously about.

Soon she stopped breathing altogether. Her eyes roll back and I knew that Dad's prediction had come about.

Life and death are apodictic with all living things and especially on a farm. I grudgingly had become accustomed to the fact that it was necessary to kill our chickens and butcher hogs and cows in order to have food on the table. Even our dogs would sometimes die as a result of an unfortunate encounter with a rattlesnake or piece of farm equipment.

But this was different. This was Ole Beauty. My charge. My friend.

ALL DAY SINGIN' AND
DINNER ON THE GROUND

Torrance County Singing Conventions took place every fourth Sunday of the month from March until August when harvest time required work in the fields even on Sundays.

Dinner on the ground was a misnomer in that it was neither dinner nor on the ground.

At midday ladies spread their best embroidered or crochet table cloths on tables set up outside the building often in the blazing sun if there were no trees to provide shade and set out their home baked casseroles, fried chicken, potato salad, "store bought" lunchmeats, and custard pies, all laid out luring swarms of flies which they warded off by swinging their dishtowels in the air over the food. This at least gave the appearance of preserving sanitation but it also meant that the cooks were usually the last to get to eat. Singing didn't diminish farm appetite so sometimes the poor gals that had done the cooking and fly swatting found little left to fill their plates.

Refrigeration was still a goal of the future as electricity in rural communities was still a footnote in the governments REA planning and only a few farmers could afford the luxury of an icebox. It is small wonder that many didn't succumb to some form of food poisoning and some may have, but I have no recollection of hearing that any of our neighbors had met such a fate. We just ate our fill, enjoyed our limited time of socializing and went on to face another day of hard work come Monday.

We were a hearty bunch.

Uncle Lester, who had a fair ear for music and a keener eye for a pretty woman, had organized the gatherings patterned after the old Brush Arbor meetings of the past. Singers who loved gospel music whether they could sing or not came from neighboring communities to listen and lend their voices. The latest Stamps Baxter song books were unboxed and distributed to the main lobby of singers.

There were duets, quartets, and a few brave soloist, all accompanied by a lone pianist, usually my cousin, Bonnie Rae or the local pastor's wife.

It was a time to fellowship, reconnect with old acquaintances and dress up in our best Sunday clothes. Ladies who could afford a new dress and hat since the last gathering sat in the rows with their red, calloused hands gloved and folded primly in their laps. Those who couldn't afford to buy a new hat usually had a newly permed hair do so all in all it was a fairly fashionable audience considering the times.

Aunt Rhoda and Bonnie Rae would have a new dress and hat. You could count on it. Mother seldom wore a hat, new or otherwise, but she had pretty hair and had learned to finger wave it so she always looked pretty but I wish she at least could have had the option of whether to wear one or not.

Aunt Rhoda and Bonnie Rae's new attire would have been ordered from the latest issue of Sears and Roebuck catalogue. Our new clothes, if we had any, were most likely sewn on our treadle Singer sewing machine which wasn't new either.

Dandelions scattered among the Daffodils.

Dad wasn't a singer but he enjoyed the music and fellowship. I was never sure whether or not Mother enjoyed either. Only later, when I matured enough to overcome being awestruck by the apparent affluence of my better dressed relatives, was I able to understand and sympathize with her reluctance to mingle with her in-laws.

When introducing us to her friends was unavoidable, Aunt Rhoda would announce with a stilted smile and dismissive wave of her hand, "These are Lester's brother's wife and children." This subtle disclaimer was obviously intended to dispel any notion that we twigs might be off-shoots from the branches of her family tree.

Mother was not immune to Aunt Rhoda's 'upishness' and hypocrisy. She was well aware that their prosperity was due in part to Dad's largess which helped boost their bank account but often left ours in the deficit column.

Mother knew and resented what I would one day come to question.

Why would a man with a large family sacrifice their needs in order to make sure his brother, with a family half the size of his, could have an easier time of it?

As much as I adored my dad, I now see this as a personality flaw.

A weakness.

Was he more concerned with their welfare than he was with ours?

Did he love them more and us less?

Why?

I wish I had asked.

Considering Mother's propensity to speak her mind whether or not it was always well timed, it must have been a real challenge for her to resist doing it during these rebukes. But she would draw her mouth into a thin line, herd us back to the table for a second helping of banana and vanilla wafer pudding and let the incident pass—at least until we were in the car on the way back home.

Once on the road she unleashed her frustration. Mimicking Aunt Rhoda's sugary voice, she would repeat the event almost verbatim. When Dad reacted in his usual nonchalant manner she reloaded for another round.

With all the surplus song books available, why was it necessary for Lester and the attractive Alto to share the same book? Was no one supposed to notice that he would curl his fingers over hers as they held the book, and did anyone else wonder why the two of them stayed in the building 'practicing' while the rest of us were outside eating?

After one of these outbursts Dad looked over and with a mischievous but knowing grin remarked, "Well, don't be so hard on him. The poor guy probably doesn't get any at home."

That seemed to settle it for Mother but it left me stumped.

What was there to get that he didn't already have? Why, they even had a player piano for goodness sake!

Years later, as an adult and able to grasp the implication of his remark, I had to admit that Dad was probably correct in his observation.

Aunt Rhoda was as rigid and straight-laced in her ideology as the stays in the corset she wore. To her way of thinking anything bordering on pleasure was considered sins of the flesh and could only be redeemed by membership and faithful attendance in the Baptist Church.

I do recall seeing her burst into laughter once. But I don't think it was on a Sunday.

Uncle Lester's womanizing and inappropriate advances were well known to all his siblings but always dismissed as "just Lester."

Even though he was quite elderly, he married a younger woman soon after Aunt Rhoda died. I never met her personally but I was told that she was an Alto singer.

THE AUSTINS AND THE AUSTINS

According to legend the generational feud between the Hatfields and McCoys was triggered by a dispute over the ownership of a hog.

No one seems to have a clear recollection of the exact cause or time that Dad's two younger brothers began their antipathy for each other and though their grievances were equally as bitter and long lasting as those of the infamous Kentucky clan, at least the animal that brought their hatred to head was of a nobler species.

The three Austin brother's homesteads were adjacent to one another with Dad's section being on the outer point of the triangle. Each had established their boundaries by stringing rows of barbed wire between wooden posts along their property lines. A portion of their acreage was set aside as grassland for their cattle. The remaining was broken out for dry land farming which consisted of corn, maze and Pinto Beans.

Over time, weather and lack of upkeep caused the fence posts to lean and become dislodged from the ground allowing the wires to sag. Cattle then were free to wander from one property to another. And they did.

It was easy enough to simply herd the stray back to its rightful owner which we did when one wandered in with our few head of cows, but Uncles Lester and Edgar would insist that the other had deliberately let the fence deteriorate or intentionally left a gate open and a ruckus between them would evolve. Occasionally a cow would invade the others bean crop and gorge on the young, green sprouts. Inevitably the rogue would bloat and die. Accusations would fly between the brothers as to who was at fault and the hostilities would exacerbate.

Blood reached a boiling point and spilled over one cold, rainy night when Uncle Lester and Vernon, Uncle Edgar's oldest son, found themselves at the same general store in the same small town.

As they were walking to their vehicles an argument broke out over one of their cows having to be put down after becoming entangled in the broken fence wire.

In the heat of anger Uncle Lester pulled out his pocket knife and stabbed Vernon several times in the abdomen. He then calmly climbed into his truck and drove home leaving his nephew bleeding on the ground.

The store proprietor rushed out, helped the wounded man to his feet and into his car. He then drove him to the local doctor's home, which also served as his office and emergency room.

The old doctor stitched him up, without the benefit of an anesthesia, and made him as comfortable as possible on a cot in his back room. He then sent a messenger to summon the only person whom he considered would be neutral in the ruckus. Dad.

The sound of a late night rain clattering on our tin roof was interrupted by a loud banging on the kitchen door.

Dad sprang from bed, hastily threw on his trousers, and taking the pistol he kept under his pillow, went to answer the door.

Following a muffled conversation he returned to the bedroom where he quickly explained to Mother where he was going. He finished dressing, pulling his overcoat on as he strode out the door and drove off into the rainy night, once again being drawn into a controversy not of his making but one which he was expected to remedy.

Not surprisingly when he heard that Dad had helped Vernon home, Uncle Lester accused him of taking sides against him, while Uncle Edgar was upset that he hadn't upbraided Uncle Lester.

No formal charges were filed by the brothers, the store owner or the doctor. Family disputes, whether settled by blade or bullet were considered to be off limits to outsiders and eye witnesses merely looked in the other direction, considering it to be a way of frontier life. But undoubtedly, they were cautious about getting into a disagreement with any of the three brothers.

An Old Timer who had become acquainted with them soon after they had settled on their properties and had no doubt heard of the wrangling that seemed to be constantly brewing between the two brothers and their respective son's, was overheard briefing a newcomer, "Them Austins is no one to mess with. They'll fight you over the sound of a rooster crowing, then turn around and beat Holy Hell out of each other."

GOOD NEWS-BAD NEWS

In 1939 spring rains coupled with the melting of the past winter's heavy snowfall provided enough moisture to officially end the drought that had ravaged the land for so long.

Our crops of beans and corn flourished but so did the weeds requiring long hours of working in the hot summer sun to keep them from crowding out the small plants. We all went to the field before sunrise. We took short breaks for the noon meal then back to work until dark. We tended to the milking, fed the pigs and chickens, ate supper by lamp light, and tumbled wearily into bed to awaken in the early morning darkness to start the process over again.

In addition to the flourishing crops, the livestock "fattened up." Market prices were fair for both.

School starting was delayed in order that students old enough and strong enough, and apparently we all were, could help in the harvest. It was a prosperous year for the farmers in our area including us. Dad was able to settle up our outstanding accounts and we enjoyed what we considered to be a rather extravagant Christmas.

We each received a new toy and new winter clothes. There was a warm winter coat for each of us and new Sunday shoes. Mine was a pair of black patent leather 'Mary Jane' high tops with buckle straps. They were only to be worn for dress-up occasions, which actually didn't happen very often.

I especially remember the little green wagon that Junior got. Some of my most nostalgic memories of him now are of putting a blanket in the bed of the wagon that spring and pulling him around the yard until he fell asleep.

That year also, we purchased a small table radio. We had no electricity but it was activated by attaching some of its connections to a car battery. Dad built a shelf for it on the wall near the kitchen stove. It was the only item of luxury we could boast of. Until now our world was primarily restricted to the confines of our farm, school, the country store and an occasional trip to town.

This little radio, no larger than a bread box brought the whole world into our tiny house.

For entertainment we had previously relied mostly on the books Dad brought home from the depository. For current events we had our Weekly Readers from school but they were pretty outdated by the time they reached us.

Now we could receive regular news updates reported by Walter Winchell. Mother listened to daytime Soap Operas; Stella Dallas, Portia Faces Life, Young Widow Brown, and others.

After dinner if our homework was finished we all sat together and enjoyed the antics of Fibber McGee and Molly, Amos and Andy, Bob Hope and Jack Benny. Other favorites were Mr. District Attorney and One Man's Family.

But one of my favorites was on Sunday. We 'tuned in' to radio station KRLD in Dallas, Texas and listened to the music of the Stamps Baxter Quartet led by the rich baritone voice of V. O. Stamps singing their theme song, "Give the World a Smile".

Basically, this was our only form of entertainment other than the games we made up which usually ended in an argument. Now things seemed more pleasant-all brought on by a small brown box that sometimes produced more static than programming.

But the same source that can provide pleasure can produce stress. It was through this medium that we learned of the Japanese attack on Pearl Harbor on an early Sunday morning, December 7, 1941.

Dad was furious. A lifelong Republican, he had become disenchanted with Hoover's failed economic programs and, blaming him for the Depression, had voted for Franklin Roosevelt and "now this S.O.B. had gotten us into war."

One would be hard pressed to locate anyone who had not been profoundly impacted by this surprise attack on our country.

Patriotism was unprecedented. The draft was quickly implemented but many farm boys eager to exchange their overalls for a military uniform didn't wait to be called up. They rushed to the Post Office which had been set up as a temporary enlistment office and volunteered for their preferred branch of service. Some lied about their age in order to get in.

A few others who were more concerned with their personal wellbeing were less enthusiastic.

Embarrassingly, one of my older cousins fit into this category. A rebel from birth, I'm told that when he was called into the enlistment office for his induction, that he defiantly stated to the Officer that he had weak ankles and that unless they agreed to allow him to wear his cowboy boots "they will just have to come and get me!"

That is precisely what 'They' did.

A couple of weeks after he failed to report for basic training, an official government car pulled into the front yard of his house. Two Military Police Officers entered the house and shortly afterward they emerged escorting my cousin between them.

He was incarcerated for a short time and when he was released he was driven to Fort Bliss in El Paso to begin his training. There he was issued a set of Olive Drab uniforms, underwear, and socks. And his boots. A pair of heavy, thick soled, G.I. combat boots with matching leggings.

I don't think he rose passed the lowest rank in the army. Even into the latter years of his life, and he lived to be elderly, he railed against the government and it's authoritarian ways.

His high school principal, who had for four years tolerated his defiant attitude, once told my dad, "That is a very smart boy." "In fact," he added, "he's too damned smart."

In contrast, another cousin drove all night to reach the nearest office of the Army Air Corp. Office, as it was known then, to enlist before he would be drafted into the regular Army. He excelled in rank and did his family proud by earning many medals and honorable commendations.

Movie Star handsome to begin with, he knocked the girls in our little town for a loop when he came home on furlough looking drop-dead handsome in his uniform.

Shortages of everything from rubber tires to certain cosmetics soon became a way of life and necessitated rationing. Each person in a family was issued a book of ration stamps that were applied to purchases. Farmers were required to burn gasoline that had been colored with a blue dye in their tractors, thus bypassing the rationing of gasoline for their cars. There was a heavy penalty imposed on anyone found using 'blue gas' in their automobiles.

Everything, it seemed, needed a ration stamp including some types of clothing. Silk stockings were replaced with rayon and it wasn't uncommon to see a well-dressed woman wearing rayon stockings with a mended run darned along the back seam of her hosiery.

We substituted Karo Syrup for sugar in our rationed coffee and on our cereal. That year there was enough sugar for my birthday cake but not for the icing. Mother iced it with peanut butter, a strange but not entirely unpalatable combination.

We finished school that year minus the high school boys that had joined the Service.

MOVING ON

Considering the low enrollment and other factors contributed to the war, a decision was made to consolidate our small country school with a larger one almost sixty-five miles away.

In order to attend that school it would have been necessary to leave home by five o'clock in the morning to catch the bus, then travel through a stretch of barren country noted for extreme weather in the winter and arrive back home after dark. This was out of the question as far as the folks were concerned so Dad decided to sell our farm and relocate near a town which was near rich irrigated farms and had one of the better accredited schools in the state.

We missed several months of school that year while Dad made successive trips to the surrounding area looking for a farm that would suit our needs and he eventually found one but there was a delay in finalizing the purchase. In the meantime he rented a place a few miles north of town as a temporary location that had enough land to hold our cattle and farm equipment.

It took several trips to transfer our belongings to the new place but the day arrived when the last items were loaded into our car and it was time to leave what had been the family home for almost seventeen years.

As we drove away, I knelt in the seat and looked out the back window. Through the swirling dust I watched our farm slowly recede into the distance.

Goodbye, house and barn. Goodbye, to my hiding places and the places where I had run and played and rolled old tires down dirt roads. Goodbye, to the rock house where I once had a playhouse. But most heartbreaking of all, because Mother firmly believed that to move a cat from one location to another would bring about the worst kind of misfortune she was adamant that Mother Cat and her litter of five kittens be left behind.

Goodbye. Goodbye.

I turned back in the seat and cried until Dad threatened to stop the car and "give you something to cry about." This was the only world I had ever known and as insecure and lonely as I had felt there at times, it still seemed more desirable than the unfamiliar destination that lay ahead of us.

I looked back once more through a blur of tears. But by now our place was out of sight. Instinctively, I knew that I was leaving not only my childhood home, but childhood itself behind.

Unless stirred by infrequent memories, such as now, I have not returned to either the place or the time which was that part of my life.

In turn, both Uncle Lester and Uncle Edgar also left their farms. Uncle Lester transferred ownership of his land to his only son and purchased several properties in Albuquerque, one being a two story rooming house which he, Aunt Rhoda and Bonnie Rae moved into occupying the ground floor. Bonnie Rae enrolled in Business College and worked part time in a law office.

Uncle Edgar deeded his farm to his two sons and moved to another county in the eastern part of the state where he passed away years later.

The bitter triangle linking the three brothers was now broken. But like some warped dynasty their respective sons continued to perpetuate the feud.

STARTING OVER

Compared to the two room house we had left behind, the new house seemed spacious. The living room had large windows that let in the morning sun and were covered with lace curtains. There were two large bedrooms which meant that we three girls would share a room and Junior would share the folk's room. It had a nice size kitchen, indoor plumbing, and a bathroom with a deep tub.

For the first time in my life I was able to read utilizing electricity rather than the dim kerosene lamps that I was accustomed to.

Mother went from room to room pointing out the uneven floors, torn window screens and worn linoleum. There seemed to be nothing that would please her short of moving back to Texas-an event that was never going to take place.

It was almost the end of the school year when Dad took us to our new school in town. My eighth grade teacher, Miss Vivian, was warm and friendly but it seemed that every eye in the classroom bore into me as we entered the room. She introduced me to the class and showed me to an empty desk. She told me to stay after class and she would supply me with the books I would need.

Self-conscious of my farm appearance, and the natural curious glances of the other kids, I spent a miserable afternoon.

Gradually I made new friends but I found it difficult to keep pace with some of the work because I had missed out on the basics taught in the beginning of the year. Math was particularly troublesome as we were getting into pre-high school algebra. But I managed to get my grades up to par and 'graduate' eighth grade in the spring.

At age twelve I was a freshman in high school. By now we had moved to the farm we had purchased and again I would need to make the transition to a new school and make other new friends.

We had moved into our new place in early May in time for spring planting. Our new house was a three bedroom log house. There was a large living room and separate dining room. One side of the kitchen had built-in cupboards and though we still used a wood burning stove, this one had a large oven and a warming oven above the top surface. The stovepipe ran through this upper oven and kept the cooked food warm until time to serve it. A screened porch ran along the back of the house. A door which was part of the porch floor opened into an underground cellar lined with shelves to hold the jars of canned vegetables, meats and jellies that we would preserve during the summer months.

Mother, Nadine, Leola and I set about unpacking and arranging the house.

Leola and I shared one of the bedrooms. Nadine had the adjoining room and Junior who was four years old now had a daybed set up in the folk's room.

There was no indoor plumbing but a well a few yards from the back door eliminated the need to haul water. We still relied on our kerosene lamps but the house had been wired for electricity in anticipation of being connected to REA later in the year.

Late one summer afternoon neighbors began arriving carrying dishes of food, cakes, Ice cream freezers and large blocks of ice. All in all about a dozen families, adults, teens and a few infants came to give us a house warming, a way of welcoming us into the community.

The men gathered around the dining room table to talk farming, discuss the war and play dominoes, each taking a turn turning the crank on the ice cream freezer. As seems to be their lot in life, the women busied themselves in the kitchen setting out the food, sharing gossip and taking turns tending to the younger children some of whom had been bedded down on the folk's bed.

We older kids gathered outside on the graveled road in front of the house to play our own games of Flying Dutchman, Two Deep, and amid shy giggles, Spin the Bottle.

In one single evening we had been warmly received into our community. Dad had already met most of the neighbors while looking for our place and greeted each arrival warmly. Mother was more aloof, and seemed determined not to enjoy the evening, complaining the next day that it would have been nice if they had bothered to let us know beforehand that they were coming. I found the entire event awesome. We had lived in virtual isolation for the twelve years of my young life and longer. Homestead farms were miles apart and the struggle to survive day to day was not conducive to socializing. Here, life was more relaxed and sociable. Hard work still prevailed but farmers gave each other a helping hand when needed. Farms were situated closer together and sometimes in the evening twinkling lights could be seen from a neighbor's house.

As it turned out these community socials were fairly routine. At least once a month on Saturday night a similar gathering took place at one neighbor's house or another.

Tragically, it was at one of these gatherings that we learned that Mrs. Morris' son, Glenn, who had dropped out of high school to enlist in the Army, had been taken prisoner and was being held in a Japanese concentration camp noted for extreme torture.

When the prisoners were liberated at the end of the war Glenn came home. He was a stooped, gaunt creature with snow white hair and walked with a decided limp, a skeletal man at twenty years of age.

There was no church building but Sunday school was held in the school house a few miles away. Dad taught an adult class and was selected to be Superintendent of the Sunday school. He arranged different level classes and persuaded some of the neighbor ladies to teach them.

Not unlike the church in our old community, there was no specific minister assigned to the area, probably because depending on the time of year, spring planting, fall harvest or adverse winter weather, attendance was unpredictable. But every few Sundays a minister from the First Baptist Church in town came out and preached a stirring sermon on the importance of "Turning your life over to Christ and having your sins washed away by being immersed in baptism."

After one particularly moving service, my best friend and I felt 'stirred' and after a brief whispered consultation with each other, we rose and followed a few other new converts to the front of the hall where we were told to kneel at a make shift alter while the minister pleaded for God's blessing to be poured into our souls.

Believing we were now sanctified, we rose from our knees and began walking back to our seats.

"Wait up there girls." It was the minister calling us back. "We need to talk with these other good people to arrange a time that's convenient for all of you to be baptized."

Suddenly I wasn't so sure I was ready for all this.

My mind went back to conversations I had heard about these community baptisms and nothing about them appealed to me.

As legend went, prior to our moving there, the stock tank on our property had customarily been the designated baptistery for the community. This tank was a relatively large rectangular concrete structure shallow enough to be waist high to the average man yet deep enough to hold enough water to allow several head of cattle to drink their fill as the water level was always near the brim. A frequently repeated account of one particular baptism was the fundamental reason for my reluctance.

Always told with the objective of getting a laugh and with each narrator applying their individual embellishments, it's difficult to know if the event even took place but I had heard it often enough for it to be believable at least in part.

One very large family who was noted for their boisterousness and irreverence had attended a church revival and had become 'born again'. But for whatever reason only the mother had decided to be baptized. This woman, as with most of her family members, was extremely obese. Reportedly, on the day of the event, with neighbors and friends gathered around the tank to witness, her two oldest sons stood on the sidelines taking bets as to how much water would be displaced when the preacher and his muscular assistant lowered her into the tank.

Added to that was my own observation of our cows leaving slobber and pieces of partially chewed cud behind when they finished drinking and suddenly the prospect of going to Hell still shackled with my unwashed sins seemed to be a reasonable alternative to me.

Finding myself in a quandary of my own making again, I looked around for Dad in the dwindling congregation. Almost as if reading my thoughts he came down the aisle and explained to The Reverend Taylor that emersion was not necessarily the only way to salvation in our belief and that I would be joining our own church denomination at a later date. As usual he was firm but diplomatic, complimenting the minister on his dedication and rousing sermon. Then, steering me ahead of him, we left the hall and were on our way home.

Keeping Dad true to his word, I did join another church a few weeks later and have remained in that denomination most of my life.

THE FIRST KISS

By now we had started to school and rather than being driven by Dad we rode the school bus. It was a nine mile ride to school so this gave us time to get acquainted with other kids on the route.

Nadine and I were the last ones to be picked up and that meant that the choice of seats usually ended up next to the driver.

J.B. Watkins was a tall boy with coal black hair and eyes. He lived with an elderly, rather reclusive uncle. I had heard that both his parents had died and that the old man had felt obligated to take him in. He had come to several of the parties and we usually managed to pair up for the games.

He saved a seat for me next to him on the bus and we rode the nine miles sitting silently and shyly, but obviously nourishing a crush on each other. He was a few years older than I , as were the rest of the kids and we had no classes to- gether but shared lunches at noon and waited side by side to catch the bus to re- turn home after school.

The last party before winter set in was held around a big bonfire at one of the houses a few miles from home and as the evening ended he asked me if he could drive me home. Of course this required getting permission from Dad.

To J.B.'s discomfort, Dad considered his request for what seemed like an eternity then reluctantly consented and drove away ahead of us.

We got into J.B.'s pickup and he drove slowly down the road. Once the tail- lights Dad's car had disappeared, J.B. pulled to the side of the road and turned off the engine. He turned toward me and told me that he had decided to join the Navy and would be leaving in a couple of weeks.

I'm not sure what my expectation had been when he pulled off the road but whatever anxiety I felt now turned to acute disappointment. Struggling to control my emotions, I said, "I don't want you to leave."

"Uncle Joe and I just aren't hitting it off." He said. "Nothing sits right with him. Everyone else is joining up and I'm going too. Maybe when this is all over, I'll be back."

With that he started the engine again and we drove the rest of the way in silence. I fought a raging battle to hold back the sadness that kept willing up in my chest.

None of the lights were on in my house as we drove into the yard and we sat for a few minutes holding hands but not speaking. Then he reached across me, opened the door and we stepped out of the truck together.

At the front door he leaned down, cupped my face in both hands and planted a lingering, awkward kiss on my lips. Without saying a word he turned and hurriedly drove out of the yard.

I stood outside the door for several minutes unable to identify my feelings but that kiss definitely left me a little breathless. It was my first real kiss and the effect must have been obvious to Mother who had watched the event through the darkened window. She flung the door open as I reached for the knob and pulled me inside. Once inside, I received her version of the ramifications of careless 'petting' which ultimately led to getting pregnant, and as usual at the conclusion of her admonishments, posed the question, "What are people going to think about you!"

Bewildered and stung by this revelation of my newest sin I went to bed and reminiscent of my childish folly and the broken light bulb at the old country store, I prayed for God's mercy.

The next time I saw my older friend, Jeanette, I asked her if she had ever kissed a boy "in a gown-up way."

"Of course." She said looking at me in astonishment.

"Well, did it make you pregnant?" I had to know. If her answer was to be the affirmative I had planned to ask her mother if I could come live with her as I was certain I would not be allowed to bring this disgrace home.

Clutching her sides, she laughed until tears were streaming down her cheeks.

"Dummy!" That's just scary stuff Mothers tell you so you don't start messing around. Kissing doesn't make you pregnant. If it did, I'd have a dozen kids running around here now. Believe me," she added wisely, "I know what makes you pregnant."

Too relieved to be embarrassed by my ignorance, I ignored her continued gales of laughter. I didn't want any further details. If kissing, messing around and getting pregnant were the natural order of things, I definitely needed to find out more about what 'messing around' was exactly. But not today. For now it was enough to know that I had escaped bringing the shame described by my mother upon myself and my family.

Mysteriously, J.B. was never heard from again after he shipped out to sea. He never returned home after the war was over. Rumor had it that he had married a Japanese girl and remained in that country. Others said he had been killed while assisting in a landing in some foreign port and one had it that he had deserted the Navy and was being held in a military prison. I doubted this one the most as I saw him to be more honorable than that.

Whatever the truth might have been seems to have been known only to J.B. and his god. But he was surely a casualty of war by whatever means.

His uncle, as far as anyone could tell, could not have cared less and died lonely and alone.

THE CONCERT

By my senior year I had become a fairly accomplished trombone player. Our band was small by comparison to others in   the state but we were well rehearsed and disciplined. We didn't dare be otherwise. Mr. Titta, our band instructor was Italian, a perfection of the highest order with a temper to match.

We had participated in several competitions with other schools in the state and each time I had been selected to play First Trombone with the top group. This was especially meaningful for me. I spent every spare minute I had rehearsing. Mr. Titta arranged to spend extra time with me during the last period of school. He coached, corrected and encouraged me and I was an enthusiastic student.

Our school had been recipient of several new band instruments earlier in the year and I was absolutely thrilled to have a new trombone assigned to me. It was a beautiful brass instrument with scroll engravings and in an elegant black leather case.

The last band activity before the end of school was a concert to be held in the local community building. Flyers advertising the event were placed in store windows and sent home with students. It was also to be a farewell tribute to Mr. Titta as he had accepted an offer to teach in a larger school.

He had chosen a variety of selections for the concert and we spent hours rehearsing, but most exciting for me was the fact that he had selected one piece that had a solo part and that part was to be mine!

I practiced that piece until I had it committed to memory. Every note was engraved on my mind. I played it for Mr. Titta over and over. Finally he advised, "No more practice. Too much playing and you lose the feeling."

The afternoon before the concert I polished my horn until it gleamed. I wiped the slide clean and worked fresh oil onto it. I placed it carefully in the case and turned my attention to my uniform, pressing sharp creases in the trousers and ironing a starched white blouse. For the first time in my life, I was confident that I would do well. This was the last time I would perform with the band and the first time my parents would hear me play.

The hall had been arranged with the band set up on a stage in the center of the floor. Metal folding chairs were set up in neat rows with the first few rows reserved for the band member's families.

We waited off stage with anticipation as the building began to fill up with parents, schoolmates and townspeople. Then led by Mt. Titta we marched two abreast and took our assigned places on the stage.

The first few pieces were military marches and folk favorites, then my piece. The entire band began to play in unison and part way through, on cue from Mt. Titta, I rose to my feet, placed the mouthpiece to my lips and began to play.

The mellow notes rose and fell as I coaxed them from the instrument. I played with confidence and pride. Not a missed note, delayed rest or overlooked repeat, blending the notes together with smooth slurs.

The piece over, I acknowledged the applause of the audience with a slight bow as Mr. Titta had instructed me to do and chanced a quick look in the direction of where my family was sitting. Amid others in the audience who were still applauding, some standing, Dad sat looking straight ahead almost expressionless and Mother was looking around nervously. Only Junior who was sitting between them was smiling and clapping.

There were a few more pieces before the concert was over but I played them by rote.

As we were putting our instruments away, Mr. Titta rushed over and greeted me enthusiastically. "Magnifico!" He exclaimed, reverting to his native language. "Perfect. Perfect. You will go far." I appreciated his kind words but the feeling of euphoria was gone now and I returned to the hall to seek out my parents among the crowd.

Riding home in the back seat of the car, I waited for an observation from Dad and hearing none, I finally asked, "How did you like the concert?"

After some thought, Dad answered. "Well, you did alright. But, " using his predictable suffix, "I don't think it was necessary to stand up and show off like that. You could have been heard just as well sitting down." Cued by Dad's criticism, I suppose, Mother now offered her own which always lasted much longer.

It would have been useless to try to explain. They had been embarrassed. It was becoming more and more evident that when it came to pleasing my parents, 'getting it right' was as elusive a goal as was finding 'Out-Of-Their-Way.'

As disappointing as their assessments were, by now they were not entirely unexpected. It was clear that my best was never going to be good enough so I salved my bruised ego by re-playing Mr. Titta's "Magnificio" over in my mind and renewing the vow I made in my childhood to make my departure as soon as possible.

Nadine had graduated a couple of years earlier and taking advantage of the male work shortage due to the war she had landed a good job in Colorado and left home to work there. Her leaving had given me a welcome reprieve from her harsh treatment and although she came back to visit from time to time, always bringing a list of demands with her, I was able to avoid her for the most part.

I reasoned that my leaving might be considered a gain. Junior had become a very real asset in helping Dad with the farm work. Only eight years old, he had learned to drive the tractor, milk, help repair broken equipment and assist with other chores. My leaving would allow Mother to dote even more attention on Leola whom she still considered to be fragile. In reality Leola had begun to show signs of becoming rebellious and incorrigible, but never mind. I hoped to soon be freed from it all.

MISS MINNIE

Two weeks before graduation I was summoned out of History class and told to report to the Principal's office.

It was common knowledge that an invitation to Miss Minnie's office, as we referred to her, was not for social reasons so I walked a little weak kneed down the hall and entered her office with no small amount of trepidation and dread. What could I have done-or not done?

She motioned for me to sit down across from her desk. Without speaking she began to arrange the papers and reports spread out before her. I glanced at her large grade book lying open and the stack of essays I had written while in her English class.

Keeping her eyes focused on me, she began to speak. "You have been a good student." She said.

Relief!

"I've reviewed your grades over the last four years and you have maintained an excellent average, especially in your writing skills. The school has a scholarship available and you have earned it. However, we need to be assured that you will be able to attend college. If not, we will award the scholarship to some other student who will be able to utilize it." "So", she continued, "discuss this with your parents and let me know their answer by Friday."

Surprised by this unexpected offer, I sat speechless. Finally, I found my voice and almost tearfully responded. "Thank you, Miss Minnie."

She nodded, smiled slightly and then, "You'd better get back to History." "By the way," she added as I reached the door, "not a word to anyone for now."

The rest of the day seemed to pass in a slow blur. I couldn't wait to get home with the news.

At the supper table, I could no longer hold back my excitement and with words tumbling over each other I told the folks about the offer.

Dad continued to eat, chewing his food slowly and deliberately while avoiding looking at me. As usual Mother began to fidget nervously looking first at Dad then back at me.

Finally, "Can I go?" I asked. "Miss Minnie needs to know by Friday."

Dad finished eating, laid his knife and fork carefully across the top of his plate and turned to look at me. He studied my face for a long moment then said, "Nadine never had a chance to go to college. We still need to help her with money. If you get to go when she didn't, she'd be upset with all of us. You'd be better off here."

My disappointment was overwhelming. For the first time that I could remember, I lashed out at my dad. "Why does everything revolve around Nadine?" I blurted out angrily. "You have other kids. Why don't we matter?" I suppose I would have continued my ranting except for the stern look on Dad's face that told me I had already gone far enough.

It took courage but I left the table with my meal half eaten and went to my room. There I cried in frustration, anger and disappointment until the early hours of morning.

The next morning, Friday, I dressed as usual noting my red swollen eyes and left the house early to await the arrival of the school bus.

After the customary morning assembly I walked slowly down the hall and knocked timidly on Miss Minnie's door.

"I'm in." She announced.

I'm sure she knew by my countenance what I was there to report, but she allowed me to give her the details while trying to hold back my tears.

She nodded occasionally and when I finished by saying, "So you see I can't take the scholarship," she rose from her desk.

"We'll see." She said.

I returned to my next class but it seemed an exceptionally long day. I looked forward to the end of the day and the weekend so I could recover from this latest, biggest disappointment of my young life.

We were up early Saturday morning as usual and went about our chores. We had just finished breakfast when there was a knock on the front door.

We exchanged questioning glances. It was highly unusual to have company this early in the day.

Dad pushed his chair back from the table and went to open the door.

To all our surprise there stood Miss Minnie.

Courteous, as always, Dad asked her in and invited her to sit down which she did and almost simultaneously began to speak.

"I'm here to make sure I understand what Anita told me yesterday." She said. And without pausing for a comment from Dad she continued, "She tells me she cannot accept the scholarship we have for her."

Still standing and a little taken aback, Dad repeated to her pretty much the same account as to why he felt I should decline the scholarship.

Miss Minnie was a spinster woman in her late fifties. She wore her salt and pepper hair bobbed in a short mannish cut and always seemed to wear the same navy blue crepe dresses and black shoes. She was a few inches shy of being five feet tall and what she lacked in stature she made up for in girth. It was a common joke whispered in the hallway at school that one could as easily jump over her as walk around her. I'm sure she was aware of these cruel remarks but rather than react to them she chose instead to concentrate on educating her classes to the best of her ability. She was firm and fair in her discipline and expected the best from her students always.

She listened attentively to Dad's explanation and when he finished, she rose to her full height and with cheeks slightly flushed she faced him and addressed him bluntly.

"A.T.", she said in a tone that she usually reserved for her most stiff-necked students. "You are an educated man and an educator yourself. I find it beyond all reason that you would deprive Anita of this opportunity to further her education because of your concern about a reaction from Nadine." She continued to speak with determination. "This has nothing to do with Nadine. Had Nadine qualified for the same offer, I assure you she would have been given full consideration. Anita has earned this opportunity not only by her grades but by her general deportment. She deserves this chance and I'm sorry to leave here knowing I will be required to award this scholarship to a less deserving student."

Dad, who was over six feet tall, stood looking down at Miss Minnie and was astonished by her boldness. The contrast of the two of them in a face-off would have been comical had they not both been so serious. He was not accustomed to having his authority challenged, especially by a woman and he was clearly uncomfortable and embarrassed. Attempting to recover but still hold his ground, he looked over at me and quickly back to Miss Minnie who had not changed her stance for a moment.

'Well," he said finally. "I'll have to study about this. I'm not sure we can afford such an outlay right now."

Before Ole Beauty had become too weak to calve she had given birth to a white face heifer which Dad had given to me as a reward for taking care of her. Over the years this young cow had also produced heifer calves and by now I had a total of five white face cows.

Emboldened by Miss Minnie championing my cause, I reminded Dad that we could sell these cows and use the money to make up the difference between the actual costs and what the scholarship would cover.

Trapped between two equally determined females, Dad hesitated only a moment longer then with a slight shrug relented.

"We'll see whether she can amount to anything or not." He said wearily.

Satisfied, Miss Minnie offered him her hand, smiled and winked slyly at me as she walked out the door.

She climbed into her old Chevy coupe and was off in a swirl of dust leaving us looking after her in astonishment.

Monday morning found me in Miss Minnie's office again. I had come to thank her for interceding for me.

"I had to give it a try." She said. Then she offered her own advice.

"Make the most of your time there." She said. "Get into a class that will further develop your writing skills. And the Arts." She added.

I assured her I would do both and as I was leaving she cautioned me again to say nothing about our discussion yet.

"We are planning an awards assembly for the students and their parents next week." She said. "We will award letters to the outstanding players on the basketball team and certificates of merit to a few other students. You will be awarded your scholarship at that time."

For a fleeting moment I felt like giving her a hug but it would have been easier to wrap my arms around a Coke machine and much less embarrassing for both of us so I resisted the impulse and left the office hoping that in her wisdom she would somehow sense my gratitude.

It was an exciting prospect to look forward to and although I longed to share my happy news with my best friend, I dared not break my promise to Miss Minnie.

The day of the assembly finally arrived and as I sat and watched the various awards being presented to my fellow classmates, I couldn't help but feel a little conspicuous and embarrassed that mine were the only parents that had chosen not to attend the ceremony. But when my name was called to come forward, I walked to the front of the room and proudly accepted my scholarship which I intended to use as a ticket.

Destination: Out-Of-Their-Way.

COUNTRY MOUSE

A few days after graduation, I approached Dad with a matter that I had been turning around in my mind for some time.

Naïve and idealistic, I felt certain that if I could get a summer job in Albuquerque, I could earn enough money to buy new clothes for college as well as set aside some spending money.

By now Nadine had quit her job in Colorado and was working in Albuquerque. She had been hired by the Police Department and was the first female to work for the department. Even though this was only a clerical position, Dad was extremely proud of her in spite of still having to pick up the tab for unpaid bills she continued to run up at a stylish dress shop.

To my surprise, Dad seemed to be expecting this. He took a few minutes to consider my request then said, "Well, I guess that would be alright, you and Nadine can room together and that way she can look after you."

Nadine? Look after me?

Now it was Dad who was being naïve. But I didn't object. I didn't want to jeopardize this opportunity and anyway, three uncomfortable months seemed a small price to pay in order to obtain my goal.

A few days later Dad drove me to town where, with suitcase in hand, I boarded a Greyhound Bus bound for Albuquerque and my job search.

Rooms were extremely difficult to come by as many military families had relocated to Albuquerque in order to be near a son or husband stationed at the base on the outskirts of the city.

Nadine had rented a room with bath in a downtown hotel on First Street across from the railroad tracks for sixty dollars a month. An unfortunate choice, as it latter turned out.

The hotel lobby was dingy, badly in need of paint, and smelled of stale cigarette smoke. The worn couches were usually filled with scruffy, shifty-eyed men who seemed to have taken up permanent occupancy on them. I dreaded walking past them on my way upstairs to our equally dingy room but I refused to be deterred. This was merely a means to where I ultimately wanted to go so I kept my eyes focused straight ahead and hurried past their stares on the way to my room.

Downtown was equally intimidating. The air was scented with the smell of exhaust fumes as cars sped by with horns blaring, protesting any impediment in traffic on their way to—wherever; a very real contrast to the clear, clean air and slow pace of life I had been accustomed to.

The day after my arrival I awoke early. Who could sleep with the constant traffic and periodic sound of a train whistle throughout the night? I dressed carefully, crossed the lobby hurriedly and set out to look for my first paying job, without, I might add the benefit of the warm, nourishing breakfast that I had become accustomed to and taken for granted at home.

Midway down Central Avenue was a large store that dealt in pottery, woven rugs and silver and turquoise jewelry all hand made by Native American Indians living on Reservations nearby. The large show case windows in the front of the store displayed these beautiful objects of art for sale at very high prices. The entryway into the store was paved with mosaic tiles in which were imbedded silver Pesos from Mexico. Inside were shelves and locked show cases filled with beautiful jewelry and pottery. The walls were covered with intricately woven Navajo rugs.

In the center of the store a large square section had been cut in the floor, the opening was covered with glass and surrounded by a waist high railing. Visitors were encouraged by a large sign that hung above the opening to "See Real Indians Making Jewelry."

By looking down from this vantage point, one could watch these workers practicing their crafts. They worked bent over under poor lighting and using crude instruments and with small torches which contributed to their discomfort due to a lack of air conditioning in what was actually the basement of the store.

A small sign in one of the windows was almost obscured by one of the beautiful pieces of pottery but as I walked by I could see it read: HELP WANTED.

I went in and approached the nearest clerk and told her I would like to apply for the job. She directed me to an area in the rear of the store where I was handed a lengthy application containing many questions that would be illegal to ask in today's society.

An official looking Store Representative quickly reviewed the application and after casually glancing up and down at me from behind his large desk, asked if I would be able to start work the following day, which of course I could.

I would be completing invoice sheets which required multiplying various figures by cost numbers all done without the aid of a machine of any kind. I would earn fifty cents an hour, work eight hours a day, six days a week without the benefit of being paid overtime for the sixth day, again a breach of today's labor laws.

I quickly made a mental calculation that I could earn almost a hundred dollars a month - big money to an inexperienced country girl.

What I hadn't considered was the amount that I would actually clear after various withholdings from my check or what it would cost me to live. Nor had I considered that Nadine would demand that I pay a larger portion of the rent since I would, as she put it, "be spending more time there than she would." She had met a handsome young man who was employed by the railroad and she was seldom around.

Discouraged but not willing to give up, I went to work the following day.

All employees were required to enter the building from a door at the rear of the store off the alley. One by one we clocked in by inserting our work cards into a time clock. No packages, other than our lunch bags or boxes were allowed. Purchases made during our lunch break were checked at the door to be retrieved at the end of the day.

Each jewelry maker was allotted a specific number of stones and amount of silver and even the tiniest stone needed to be accounted for at the end of each day. They were required to empty their pockets at the end of each shift, presumably, in the event some might be trying to smuggle out a few stones.

Restroom breaks were scheduled and timed. Should there be a delay in returning from the restroom, a supervisor soon came to see what was causing the delay.

We invoice clerks were given a pencil without an eraser as it was expected that mistakes would not be made. We were responsible for this pencil and a request for a new one was denied if the one being used was still long enough to be sharpened.

The exploitation of workers both Indian and non-Indian is hard to imagine in today's workplace. But this type of treatment didn't seem to be out of place at the time. Nevertheless, it seemed to me even then, that the unfair treatment of the Indian workers in particular, could in no way be justified and yet they seemed to accept it with a good deal of tolerance. Stranger still was the fact that the proprietors of this store was a family who themselves had emigrated from their native country in the Middle East possibly to escape just such unjust treatment. But they had grown very wealthy in America and perhaps their success had erased the memory of their past misery.

I walked the five or six blocks to and from work each day sometimes in awe of the sights and sounds around me. I paused occasionally on the way back to my room to look in the window of a dress shop imagining the time when I would actually be able to begin shopping for my new clothes.

My first pay check was disappointingly small, as were the following ones. By the time I gave Nadine my share of the rent, there was very little left to live on. By skipping breakfast I usually managed a fairly decent lunch. But dinner, more often than not , consisted of Spam and soda crackers which I ate alone in the room.

At bedtime I took a bath in the stained bathtub, braced the door shut with the only chair in the room, which made Nadine furious on the rare occasions when she did come in for the night, and climbed wearily into bed. I slept uneasily, always aware of the sounds coming from the street below and the hallway and adjoining rooms.

It is doubtful that a more accurate personification of a Country Mouse attempting to acclimate to life in the city could have been found. Still I persisted in pursuing my goal of earning enough money to buy a nice wardrobe for college.

By leaving the hotel early in the morning, I was able to avoid the stares and coarse remarks of the riffraff that drifted in throughout the day to smoke cigarettes and swap crude jokes as they lounged on the soiled couches in the lobby. Additionally, I could make certain that I would arrive at work early enough to check in on time. Even being five minutes tardy was not tolerated and every employee was aware that their job was at risk if they checked in late, so often there was a group in the alley waiting for the store to open by the time I got there.

I performed my job duties perched on a high stool under a dim electric light that hung above the table. There were no clocks on the walls. The end of the day was signaled by a loud buzzer that could be heard throughout the basement.

At the end of the day, I stepped down from the stool, clocked out and was never surprised to see that the clock on the bank building across from the store always showed a time thirty minutes later than the setting on the clock we used to stamp our time cards.

I walked the same few blocks back to the hotel but sometimes I would stop at the dress shop and browse through the sale rack, once managing to purchase a skirt and sweater at a reduced price.

A RUDE AWAKENING

It was Sunday. All the department stores were closed so instead of strolling down Central Avenue to window shop, I walked to a nearby newsstand and bought a Coney Island Hot Dog and a True Story magazine with the leftover change.

The hotel lobby was empty when I entered the front door. The miscreants had vacated their couches in search of a cool place to hang out in a nearby park or more likely to panhandle at the railway station across the street.

Their absence provided me with the opportunity to leave the door to my room slightly ajar in hopes of capturing some air that might be circulating through the hall.

I had just filled a glass of water from the tap in the bathroom when I heard a couple of quick taps on the door.

Startled, I turned and was surprised to see Uncle Lester stick his head in the door. Seeing me there he came in without being invited and closed the door behind himself.

He was dressed in his Sunday clothes, obviously having attended late church services.

Noting the surprise on my face, he said, "I just wanted to see if you girls were doing alright."

Moving further into the room he noticed the magazine lying on the bed and reached for it. He flipped through a few pages then turned to me and said "Girl, you don't need to read this junk to find out how to have a good time."

He sat down on the bed, pulled me down to sit beside him and cupped his hand over my bare knee. He was wearing his gold ring with his Thirty-Third Degree Masonic emblem imbedded in the ruby cabochon.

His voice was husky as he put his face next to mine and whispered, "Can you keep a secret with me?"

Warning bells began to toll in my head.

I pulled away and stood up. I needed to get away from this uncle that had now become a repugnant, frightening stranger.

My mind raced. How to get out of this room?

"Let's go to your house and check on Aunt Rhoda." I said, grasping at the only thing that came to my mind as a way to get away from him.

He got to his feet, straightened his tie and suit jacket, "That's a good idea. It certainly will be cooler there than in this stuffy room."

Relieved, but still shaken, I followed him out of the hotel into the hot afternoon heading in the direction of his house a few blocks away.

I kept as much distance between us as possible as we walked along the hot sidewalk crowded with people on their way home or rushing to catch the last bus of the day.

At least it hadn't been difficult to persuade him to leave the hotel on the pretext of checking on Aunt Rhoda. In fact, I hadn't needed to persuade him at all. He seemed pleased that I had suggested we go to his house.

Then it struck me. Maybe Aunt Rhoda wasn't home!

Was I walking into the Devil's Den?

In a panic I turned and began to run back toward the hotel. I ignored their harsh scolding as I collided with the crowd.

A taxi driver slammed on his brakes and shouted an obscenity as I sprinted across the street ignoring the traffic signal.

The clerk at the front desk of the hotel glanced around curiously as I raced through the lobby and up the stairs to my room.

Using the rusty key, I locked myself in, shoved the chair in front of the door and fell across the bed exhausted.

Soaked in perspiration and with my heart pounding, I buried my face in the pillow and cried in frustration, confusion and outrage.

Was there something in my persona that brought out the dark side of my family toward me?

Was this really the world which I had been so eager to venture into?

Would I always be running away from something or someone?

Maybe this was what Dad had been alluding to when he counseled me to be "tough as a rabbit."

Without turning off the overhead light I crawled under the covers still wearing my clothes and fell into a troubled sleep.

It was three o'clock in the morning. I awoke to the sound of someone pushing angrily on the door. My heart raced as I watched a hand reach through the slight opening and shove the chair over.

Nadine stood in the doorway. She had come to pick up a change of clothes and was livid to find the door blocked.

I covered my head with the pillow again to block out her ranting and when she was gone, slamming the door loudly as she left, I got up and took a long hot bath in the dingy tub.

I dressed and sat on the side of the bed to wait for daylight so I could leave for work.

It would be another terribly long day.

Fortunately, for me at least, sales at the store had picked up. The increase in inventories kept us busier than usual and the supervisors even more short tempered so the days were filed with extra work and no extra hours added to complete it so there was little time to brood.

I had contemplated but quickly dismissed the idea of confiding in Nadine. She would have scoffed or accused me of lying and I didn't need to hear her lecture.

There was no convenient way to let Dad know even if I had felt comfortable in telling him so I dismissed that thought as well; and anyway as far as Uncle Lester was concerned, I had just learned to "stay out of his way!"

Gradually, I was able to stop reliving the incident which had played over in my mind like a needle stuck in the groove of a phonograph record.

Though Dad was larger in stature, he and Uncle Lester had facial resemblances and I had always respected him. Now I felt only disgust and repulsion when he came to mind.

He and Aunt Rhoda seem to have had the notion that being poor somehow diminished our worth as human beings and I resented it.

Afflicted since youth with intermittent bouts of pellagra, Uncle Lester began experiencing the effects of the disease as he aged.

Realizing his vulnerability he made an effort to contact Uncle Edgar to reconcile their differences. Only then did he learn that Edgar had passed away years earlier without as much as mentioning his brothers name.

When Lester passed away a few years later the Sunshine Quartet replaced him with another tenor and at his funeral they sang one of the gospel songs he had written.

With the pride and emphasis they put on the value of possessing material belongs,   I'm sure that after the services some family member removed the Masonic ring and Shriners pen he was wearing for display.

But he took his hypocrisy and deviant sexual appetites to the grave with him along with my resolve not to divulge his sick 'secret'—until now.

INTERRUPTED PLANS

In spite of the lonely evenings spent alone in my room, there was a certain feeling of excitement of being on my own in a big city.

The city seemed to throb with a life of its own. I was impressed by the business appearance of well-dressed men and women entering tall professional buildings in the mornings and exiting them in the afternoon. They walked hurriedly and with a purpose. They drove away at the end of the day in nice, shiny cars and I supposed to beautiful, well-furnished homes. I imagined myself being part of this group—someday.

For now though I would have to be content with where I was in my life and wait.

There were only a few weeks left before I would be leaving for college so I persevered onward.

It was late summer and I couldn't remember when the heat had been so stifling. Hugging the buildings in order to walk in the shade offered little relief.

It was a real certainty that the room back at the hotel would be sweltering at this time of day as well. There were no windows and the only door opened into the hallway which wasn't any better.

I decided to stop at the store where I had some things on layaway and make a payment and perhaps linger a little longer than necessary to absorb some cooling relief from their air conditioner.

Long minutes later, I walked into the hotel lobby and heard loud voices at the front desk.

Nadine and the hotel manager were in the midst of a heated argument.

"You pay bill or I keek your skinny asses to the street!" he was shouting.

Nadine, just as adamant, was shouting back that he dare not touch us.

What in the world I wondered?

I glanced around at the captive audience of rummy characters occupying the couches enjoying the spectacle.

From the corner of my eye I caught sight of a tall figure entering the front and taking long strides toward the desk.

Dad!

As if by divine providence he had been in town and had come to check on us before returning home. God knows his arrival couldn't have been better timed.

He walked passed me and directly to the counter where he positioned himself between Nadine and the manager.

"What seems to be the problem here?" He asked.

The manager was a skinny runt of a man with jaundiced skin. The grease on his hair had seeped into the edge of his shirt collar. He had small dark eyes centered too close to the bridge of his nose. In the couple of months that I had been there I had never seen him in a change of clothing and he reeked of body odor. He was obnoxious and rude if we spoke to him about a problem with the room, always playing to his couch audience.

 Now confronted by what must have seemed to him a Goliath, his demeanor changed completely.

He stepped back, and smiling through cracked, yellow teeth he answered in broken English. "Well, you see, kind Sir, theeze nice young ladies here seem to have overlooked zee rent. Zhey have been given nice room but no pay for. I merely try to make arrangement."

"These nice young ladies," Dad interrupted mockingly, "are my daughters. If they say they have paid, they've paid."

"But kind Sir—." Dad interrupted him again but this time he directed his attention to Nadine.

"Do you owe this man money?"

Nadine who was as surprised as I at having Dad suddenly appear from nowhere, lowered her eyes, "No." She said, lowering her voice considerably. "We've paid every penny."

"No." Again the manager attempted to protest but meekly backed away when Dad raised his hand indicating the discussion was over.

"Get your things," Dad told us. "You are not staying here any longer." My heart sank. Nadine wouldn't have any problem finding another place. She already spent most of her time with an older woman who owned a rooming house across the street from where her male friend lived. But I didn't know anyone.

As we put our things in the car, Dad said to me, "You are coming back home with me."

"But what about my job?" I wanted to know.

"You are coming home with me." Dad repeated.

Past experience had taught me that there was nothing to be gained by further protests. He had made up his mind and that was that.

So without giving notice to my employer or having the opportunity to pick up the sweaters that I had on layaway at the dress shop, I found myself riding beside Dad on the way back home.

Once we were out of traffic and well on the road, Dad turned to me and asked, "Did you girls, or did you not pay that man his money?"

I explained that I had always given Nadine my share of the rent and she was supposed to have paid.

Dad studied my face for some time. Then sighing, he shook his head rather sadly and continued to drive on.

Honest to a fault, he must have been disappointed and discouraged to have had our integrity questioned. But he too, must have had questions as to what the true facts were.

Actually I wasn't positive whether Nadine had paid or not. But we both knew Nadine.

As was his nature, Dad never brought the matter up again, but even now, one of my regrets is that he was put in the uncomfortable position of wondering about our honesty. By virtue of his own example, he must have been hurt to think either of us would compromise his teachings and I'm sorry he was faced with this doubt.

Going back home wasn't all that bad, I discovered. It felt secure to be back around familiar things and Mother's country cooking had never tasted so good.

I was let down by having to acknowledge that my summer had amounted to less than I had envisioned it was going to be but there was still a few weeks left before I would leave for college.

Whereas our farm consisted of growing Pinto Beans, corn and alfalfa, one of the irrigated farms that adjoined ours was mostly devoted to growing vegetables such as sweet corn, carrots and peas.

By this time the peas were ready to be picked for market. The farmer was paying picker's one dollar for each bushel picked so I signed on. I still had hopes of earning extra money for school.

It required kneeling in the mud to hand pick the peas from the vines. The work was hard and the days were long and hot but by the end of the week all the crop had been gathered and I had earned enough to buy some fabric to make a few clothes.

A dollar could buy four yards of fabric at a small store in our town. This was more than enough for a dress, so with my earnings, I felt I had done fairly well and resigned myself to be satisfied with what I had-at least for now.

Only later did I realize that no college curriculum could have offered a more enlightened course in what real life was about than the lessons I had learned while spending those few weeks alone in a strange city in the summer of 1946.

THE FIRST STEP

WELCOME TO NEW MEXICO HIGHLANDS UNIVERSITY FRESHMAN WEEK

A large banner printed with purple letters on a white background was stretched between two main buildings on the college campus.

Incoming freshmen had been instructed to arrive a week prior to the beginning of the fall semester for orientation which included pre-college testing, class registration and in general given an opportunity to meet with professors and counselors and become familiar with the campus layout. Social 'mixers' were also included in order that we could meet other freshmen.

The catalogue that had arrived a month or so before the beginning of the fall term had listed the items that would be required to furnish the dorm rooms: Two sets of twin size sheets and pillowcases. One bed spread, two bath towels, two face towels and four wash clothes. Other than clothing we were discouraged from bringing other personal belongings.

Each room would accommodate two people and a set of dorm rules was outlined and would be strictly enforced. Rooms were to be kept clean at all times and would be inspected daily by one of the two 'House Mothers'. Failure to abide by this rule was punishable by a warning for the first offense; grounding for a weekend for the second and confined to campus for the third. No male visitors were allowed past the front waiting area and if some daring soul managed to sneak one into her room and was caught she was expelled from college.

Meals were served family style at specific times in the dining room three times a day but the dining room was closed after the noon meal on Sunday leaving us to manage on our own for the evening.

These meals, as it turned out, were as unimaginative as they were predictable.

Monday's menu was repeated on the following Monday as were those of each successive days of the week and the choice of Tuesday's dinner of Franks and Beans was definitely not made in consideration that the girls' basketball games were also scheduled on Tuesday nights I was to realize.

We soon learned that the sharp pains we were experiencing by half-time were not bruised ribs inflicted by the opposing team, but rather acute indigestion.

Dorm hours were posted at the front desk. All residents must in their rooms by 10:00pm Sunday through Thursday. These hours were extended to 11:00pm on Fridays and 1:00am on Saturday.

Absolutely no alcohol was allowed on the campus.

These rules seem archaic by today's standards of 'no rules' but this was 1946. Now puritan ethics pretty much dominated the attitudes and as far as I know there were few infractions. Ours was an unspoiled generation disciplined by the harshness of an economic depression and tempered by war. It would be left to future generations to challenge authority with demonstrations and disruptive behavior.

My roommate and her mother were busily unpacking her things and arranging her clothes in her closet and chest of drawers when I entered the room. They interrupted their work to introduce themselves.

Dottie Sloan was a chubby, dark hired, round eyed girl with a bright smile and outgoing personality, She and her mom had arrived earlier and were almost finished setting up her side of the room.

Mrs. Sloan continued hanging clothes in the closet while Dottie and I began to get acquainted. It was obvious that her wardrobe was much more extensive than mine as her mother continued to struggle to push the hangers into her crowded closet.

"Dottie, you are just going to have to keep some of your things in your footlocker," she interrupted our conversation. "There is no more space in this closet."

It was a sure thing I would not share her problem. But I was accustomed to having a sparse wardrobe and I spent extra effort in making sure my clothes were spotlessly clean and neatly pressed so I wasn't really fazed by this.

I noticed several stuffed animals propped on her bed along with extra pillows.

I had owned a few dolls in my childhood but couldn't remember ever having a stuffed animal and wondered if bringing them to college, despite the rules, was even appropriate. Still something about them did make her side of the room appear less spartan and more cheerful.

"Well, dear," Mrs. Sloan nodded to Dottie, "Dad is waiting outside. You can finish up. Walk out with me and tell your father goodbye." She gave me a brief one armed hug and together they left the room.

I sat on the side of my unmade bed and felt a surge of melancholy sweep over me. This girl and her mother seemed to share such camaraderie, almost as if they were the same age. I found myself wishing that my mother had come. I knew she had wanted to and had planned to, but Nadine had quit her job with the police department and had come home for an indefinite period of time, complaining of some unexplained illness and needing rest.

When she had learned that I would soon be leaving for college she was furious. Turning her rage on Dad, she demanded to know why I was allowed to go when everyone knew she was smarter by far than I was. Actually this was true. She was much quicker to grasp new knowledge than I was and she didn't seem to need to study as hard as I did to make good grades.

Dad attempted to placate her by offering to send her now but the thought of entering college as a freshman along with me was too much for her narcissistic ego and she refused to consider it, choosing instead to assume the role of being overworked to the point of exhaustion and expecting Mother to cater to her needs.

So when the day came for us to leave, Dad and I packed my things in the trunk of the car and left on a crisp September morning to begin the first leg of my journey to Out- Of-Their-Way.

We drove the several hundred miles mostly in silence. As always the awkwardness I felt when I was alone with Dad took over. The nearer we came to reaching our destination, the more apprehensive I became. Maybe this wasn't going to work out after all. Maybe Nadine was right and I wasn't smart enough for college. But turning back seemed even bleaker.

I knew it wouldn't take much for Dad to change his mind, scholarship or no scholarship so I kept my doubts to myself. Still, it was with no small amount of unease that I watched him drive away after unloading my things in the front waiting room of the dorm.

I was sixteen years old and as it turned out, would be the youngest student on the campus.

I had just finished making my bed when Dottie breezed back into the room with a cheery "Hi" and set about rearranging her things again. She laid out a black dress with a full skirt across her bed then turned to me, "The Mixer is tonight. Do you mind if I use the shower first? Did you bring a dress for the dance? Eddie Marensick's band is playing."

No, I didn't mind. Yes, I had the dress.

"Who is Eddie Marensick?"

"He's a sophomore from my hometown. He and some of his buddies organized a small band. He's really very good. You'll love him," from behind the closed bathroom door.

As we dressed for the dance Dottie kept up a steady prattle of conversation. She was an only child and obviously enjoyed the indulgence of her doting parents. By the time we were ready to leave the room I felt I had a complete history of her life and family. She hadn't asked and I didn't volunteer anything about mine.

The student ballroom was in the west wing of the same building that housed the girl's dorm and was separated from the dining hall by a long corridor. It had been decorated with streamers and balloons in the school colors of purple and white. A large banner behind the band read: WELCOME NMHU FRESHMEN. The dance band could be heard warming up and several students were chatting in small groups as we entered the room.

This year's freshmen enrollment was the largest in several years due to the return of servicemen who would be attending on the G.I. bill.

The band led by Eddie Marensick on the trumpet opened the dance with his theme song, "Stardust". Dottie had not been exaggerating. He was good. A more comparable sound to that of Harry James would have been hard to find.

Soon partners were dancing to the swing of the music and to an outside observer, it would have been difficult to believe that only a few minutes earlier we were all strangers.

We danced, pausing occasionally for a break at the refreshment table for punch and cookies, and as the evening wore on I gradually lost my self-consciousness and shyness. Somewhere in my young life I had learned to appreciate the rhythm of music and was a good dancer. To the best of my memory I didn't sit out a single dance that evening and when it ended at midnight had made many new acquaintances.

The dance ended with Eddie playing his theme song again and as we were leaving to return to our dorms some of us agreed to meet as a group after breakfast the following day, Sunday, to explore the town.

Back in our room, Dottie resumed her chatter, elaborating on the dance and how much fun she had had, the boys she had an eye on and hoped to date, and how exciting college was going to be.

I kept pretty mum but felt a degree of excitement myself. Several of my dances had been with a tall, good looking boy named Windell Scarbrough. He lived in town and had asked to meet me the next day to show me around.

It was easy to make friends here. For the most part we were all pretty much on equal status. Of course there were some students who were from affluent homes and backgrounds but they were the minority. The returning G.I.'s were a few years older than the high school graduates and seemed more serious but generally speaking we were a compatible group of diverse individuals with a common goal.

I fell asleep that night with the reservations I had previously felt about being here subsiding and intermittent refrains of "Stardust" drifting in and out of my sleepiness.

Only registered residents of the dorms were allowed to eat in the dining room so Windy was waiting outside on the steps when I finished breakfast. I signed out and we began our tour of the campus and town.

Having lived here most of his life, Windy was familiar with the campus and pointed out the various academic buildings, library, music hall and auditorium. Comparatively speaking this was a small university and was run almost like a private school. Rules that would be impossible to impose on campuses today were in effect and unquestioned.

I later learned that the Dean of women had established a dress code for all female students.   No slacks in the classroom. Blue Jeans could not be worn on campus unless a special   sports event required them. She taught English Literature and had a regal air about her. She came to class dressed to the nines. Seldom was she seen wearing the same dress twice and always had a matching hat. One hat that she wore was particularly   bothersome to me. It was a large brimmed 'picture' hat covered with millions of tiny yellow feathers which I was told had been plucked from canaries. I never knew for sure, but was told that she never removed her hats because she was bald. She was a commanding figure with a great deal of influence on the rest of the faculty. Kennedy Hall, the girl's dorm, was so named in her honor.

After touring the campus Windy and I walked to the main street of the town and to the Home Café for lunch which as it turned out was a favorite   place for students to hang out. We ended the day at a small park sitting on benches and exchanging talk on how we planned to spend our college days. He wanted to be a teacher and would major in education. He seemed surprised that I was interested in Journalism since almost everyone who came here, came seeking a degree in teaching. He explained that until recently this University had been dedicated exclusively to offering courses in teaching and had also recently changed its name from New Mexico Normal Teachers College to New Mexico Highlands University.

We walked back to the dorm together, said goodbye at the door and promised to keep an eye out for each other between classes. Tomorrow would be a full day of class assignments and meeting with counselors.

It was still early and Dottie wasn't back in the room yet. I sat down at the desk and wrote my first letter home.

TAKING A BIG BITE

Class registration took up most of the day Monday and was another new experience for me. The small school that I had graduated from did not require pre-registration. Subjects were assigned according to grade level with the degree of difficulty advancing as one progressed from grade to grade and all subjects were required courses as determined by the State Accrediting Board. There were no elective courses and one must successfully pass all classes in order to graduate.

I finished meeting with the last professor in mid-afternoon and headed to the college book store. I located the books I needed and found that if I bought used books I could get them at a good, reduced price, another revelation as our books had been furnished in high school.

The dining hall that evening was buzzing with talk about class room numbers and warnings from the sophomores who, with classic wisdom, advised us how to relate to various professors if they had been in their class the previous year. We were told that some instructors were eccentric 'hard asses' who assigned home-work as if theirs was the only class you had registered for. Others were more reasonable and even others sometimes failed to show up on occasion. But above all we were told that it was imperative to take copious notes as we would need to rely on them when exams came around.   None of this talk helped to assuage the anxiety most of we freshmen were already feeling.

The first week of classes took some adjusting to, but I soon became familiar with the routine of changing rooms, sometimes between buildings, and realizing that I did not always have the same class every day.

Student mail boxes were located outside the dining room and mail was deliv-ered and distributed in late afternoon. As yet I hadn't received a letter from home. I knew this was harvest time on the farm and thus there was very little time for letter writing but still I checked my box each time I left the hall hoping to find an envelope with Dad's familiar handwriting . Instinctively, I suppose, I didn't expect to hear from Mother. Not surprisingly, Dottie received mail almost every day, sometimes in the form of comical greeting cards which she taped to her closet door. Periodically her mail along with that of some of the other students would contain cash sent by their parents for extra spending money. No one ever complained of missing their mail which seems unbelievable today especially since the boxes were mere pigeonholes mounted on the wall. What a difference a generation can make.

My Journalism Professor had given me an assignment as a feature writer for the college newspaper which was published bi-monthly. And it was necessary to spend hours after my last class seeking interviews and finding interesting subjects to write about. My other classes required spending considerable time in the library as well and I was unaccustomed to the pace and seemingly endless shuffling between class rooms, library and the dorm.

But life on campus was not entirely restricted to classroom work, I learned. There was Freshman Orientation Week, pep rallies, Saturday night dances and Fraternity and Sorority Rush Weeks.

Several evenings after dinner a representative from one of the several sororities would visit our room, and in what could be compared to political lobbying, attempted to 'sell' us on the advantages of belonging to her particular group. Dottie decided to pledge Delta Delta Delta, more commonly referred to as Tri Delta which was strictly social and had a membership of mostly well-to-do girls who could afford the stiff dues. I joined Delta Sigma Epsilon which was more dedicated to local charity and educational interests. But even though the dues were more reasonable than some of the others, I knew Dad would consider belonging to one at all to be frivolous so I took advantage of an opening I had heard about and went to work in the Comptroller's office in order to pay the monthly dues.

Life here was a huge pie and I was biting of bigger and bigger pieces.

Without realizing it I was beginning to fall behind in my studies. I was unaccustomed to the whirl of social activities I had allowed myself to get swept up in.

Foolishly, I took up smoking cigarettes partly because the more sophisticated girls all smoked and partly because I thought it would deflect some of the teasing about being the "baby on the campus".

College was a fast moving train and I was standing squarely in the middle of the track.

By the end of the first quarter when grades were posted and, to my consternation, mailed home, mine were disappointingly low. Journalism and Art were the only subjects that I received a grader higher than a C+ and I felt totally defeated.

A week later when I checked for mail I was not disappointed. The envelope addressed with Dad's perfect penmanship was sitting ominously in the slot.

It had become routine for students to gather at the mail station after dinner each day to pick up and read their mail while sitting in groups on the dorm steps. Often they shared their letters with each other, laughing and chatting about news from home. Until now I had not had reason to join this group but I had a sixth-sense that this first letter from home was not one I would want to share.

My intuition had not failed me. Alone in my room I read Dad's letter. He sternly informed me that it was costing almost a thousand dollars a month (a considerable amount in 1946) to keep me in school. Without mincing words, he reminded me that I was "never going to amount to anything" if I couldn't do better than what these grades indicated I was doing. It was a long letter of reprimands, expressed disappointments and comparisons to the grades I had achieved in high school. He closed by reminding me that I could be put to good use on the farm if I couldn't do better in school.

I read the letter again and again as if the harsh words could somehow be honed down by repeated readings. I remembered the doubts he had expressed about my ability to 'amount to anything' when Miss Minnie had come to persuade him to let me attend college, and to further torture myself, I recalled the last meeting in her office-"make the most of your time there-" I had not only let the two of them down but myself as well.

There was a two week break between quarters. With the exception of the out of state students and those with part time jobs off campus, most of the students went home during this time. This left the dorm virtually empty and only a few tables in the dining hall utilized.

Not having bus fare to go home, I was one of five girls left in the dorm. I was determined to use this time of virtual solitude to regain my focus and made a plan to better organize my time by eliminating some extra curricula projects which I had unwisely become involved in and concentrate on my studies.

By completing my assignments at the library rather than in my dorm room with its interruptions and distractions, I found I was able to complete the work more timely. I avoided the hang-outs where students gathered after classes and used that time instead to concentrate on art projects.

Unable to completely forgo my love for dancing, I allowed myself the treat of an occasional Saturday night mixer but for the most part I kept my nose to the grind stone and the letter from Dad tucked in the inside slot of my notebook.

By the end of the second quarter I had regained my academic equilibrium and had no qualms about my grades being sent home.

Evidence that they had proven to be acceptable there was the absence of a letter from Dad this time. It was not his practice to commend or praise work that was no more than what one was capable of doing so this wasn't unexpected on my part.

I completed my term as a Feature Writer for the paper and was given an assignment on the editorial staff which was more work but not as interesting as a freelance writer. Journalism was only a two year course at this university at this time so the various facets of working for a newspaper were crammed into a short period of time.

My art class which was titled "Art of Expression" was just the opposite. Mr. Horn was a lay-back professor who didn't give specific assignments regarding subjects to be drawn, or in my case done with water colors, but instead as the title suggested, let us choose our own subjects in which to express ourselves.

My first attempts were still life pieces and though, unconsciously usually of food. There was the customary but trite picture of fruit overflowing from a wicker basket, and another of a large banana split with chocolate syrup dripping over the edge of the dish.

"Are you always hungry? Mr. Horn joked as he observed my work.

This class was the last one before lunch break so I suppose he could have had a point, but a more accurate observation, I think, was that my imagination was limited by having had so little exposure to various types of art.

The fourth quarter of this class was dedicated to painting with oils but in the meantime, Mr. Horn had announced that one of the Fine Art Galleries in Santa Fe had offered to exhibit several pieces of work from students in his class as a way of encouraging aspiring artists. The pieces would be juried by an independent group of artists from the gallery and monetary prizes would be awarded for the best three.

I submitted several of my pieces and was ecstatic when Mr. Horn selected one to be juried. I had sketched   then painted a picture of a girl sitting on a grassy mound with her back leaning against the trunk of a large leafy tree. Her knees were drawn up and she was resting her head on her arms folded across her knees. She wore a pleated skirt, 'Sloppy-Joe' sweater and white saddle shoes. Her white socks were turned down in thick folds above her ankles as was the style on campus that year. A book with a page fluttering in an imaginary breeze lay open at her feet.

My painting did not win one of the prizes but I felt rewarded that it had been selected to be reviewed by a distinguished panel.   I was especially proud to note that it had been officially stamped and dated as having been exhibited at a well-known art gallery. I carefully placed it in a tube and mailed it home.

At home for Thanksgiving break, I inquired about the painting and was told that Nadine had "accidently" overturned a glass of water on the dining room table where the painting had been spread out to flatten after having been rolled in the tube.

I didn't buy the story but at least I had learned, finally, not to let her spiteful actions take the emotional toll on me that they once had done. By now I realized that it would ever be thus as long as we shared the same small world that we referred to as home.

I finished my freshman year satisfied with my grades and progress and went home for the summer. I had hoped to get a paying job in order to earn money for the fall term but Dad needed help in the field so I spent the summer there instead.

Fortunately for me, Nadine had made a miraculous recovery from her 'debilitating' illness and had returned to work. She managed to secure a job with the railroad again and had moved away from home one more time. But not for the last time by any means. Her leaving only to return again was a behavior that she repeated ad nauseam until Dad passed away twenty-eight years later. She sincerely believed and somehow had convinced him, that merely by virtue of birth order she was entitled to receive special favor.

And she usually did.

OIL AND WATER

I entered my sophomore year that fall with three things being certain in my mind. One, I needed to take as many credit courses as I could carry that would enhance my studies in Journalism. Two, this would be my last year as money was scarce again and I knew I could not expect more from home. Even though she had a full-time, well- paying job, Nadine still made demands for and received help from the folks which put a drain on them financially, and number three, I was probably the only female on campus with farmer calluses on her hands. And probably, subconsciously, there was a fourth. I must find a means to reach "Out-of-Their-Way." The thought of returning home permanently was not something I was willing to accept.

Dottie and I were assigned a room together again and after spending an hour or so hearing her relive how she spent her summer break, we set about unpacking and arranging our sides of the room. Even though we had very little in common, I did not find her to be an unpleasant person. We were compatible and got along well together but outside of sharing the same room, we had very little to do with each other off campus.

Mr. Lancaster, the journalism instructor, suggested that in order to learn the newspaper business from the ground up I should spend some time observing the actual publishing of a newspaper. So I called the editor of the local newspaper and arranged a time to spend the day observing the process.

The editor/owner was a middle aged man, friendly but not too talkative. His hands and nails were permanently dyed with ink from manually setting type. I watched without benefit of explanation as he set up the type for the next day's headlines. As the day progressed I saw the paper move through the various stages of being printed and readied for delivery the following morning.

I loved the smell of the printers ink and the sound of the presses but by the end of the day I was certain that that part of the newspaper business would be well off left to others. I would not be a hands-on newspaper publisher. I wanted to write.

I spent most of the following day at the library. It was 6:30 Friday evening. I closed the reference book and snapped the sheet of note paper back into my notebook.   I had decided to skip dinner in the dining hall, electing instead to spend time getting a head start on next week's assignments. Saturday was kick-off day for Homecoming activities and I intended to participate.

It was beginning to get dark as I walked across the campus to the dorm. Miss Frazier, one of the House Mothers, was sitting in the waiting room and noticing me struggling to open the door and balance an armload of books, came to hold the door open.

"Wait." She said as I thanked her and walked past her on the way to my room. "A special delivery letter came for you today." She was having difficulty restraining her curiosity as she handed me the letter.

Curious and anxious as well, but not willing to share what I intuitively suspected was unpleasant news from home with this nosey woman, I took the letter and hurried down the hall to my room.

I spilled the books on my bed and hastily tore open the envelope addressed in Dad's unmistakable handwriting.

Inside a single sheet of folded paper was a ten dollar bill and a hastily written note.

Nadine had met a fellow railroad employee in the small town where they were stationed about a hundred miles from the university and they were getting married this upcoming Saturday, tomorrow. He and Mother did not plan to attend but he felt someone in the family should go. The money was for bus fare. I viewed this as more of a directive than a request. I grudgingly laid the letter on my desk and relinquished my plans to join in tomorrow's pep rally

Why Me?

Saturday I caught the early morning Greyhound Bus bound for Amarillo, Texas and settled back for the hour and half ride to its first stop in Vaughn where Nadine and her prospective husband lived and were going to meet me.

As much as I was not looking forward to the day's events, I still found myself hopeful that at least maybe she was finally going to build a life of her own and cease her demands on the folks.

Jim Lockhart was a heavy set, blading man considerably shorter than Nadine's six feet. He was slightly myopic, walked with a slouch and there was almost a timid air about him.

Nadine, on the other hand, was her usual domineering self, hurrying us along to have lunch and get our clothes changed before we went before the Justice of The Peace for the ceremony.

We ordered the Today's Special from the menu at the only café in town, a small restaurant on Main street with a long counter with stools and a half dozen tables covered with worn red checkered oil cloth and a heavy odor of cooking oil permeating the room.

Between bites of food I learned that Jim had been with the railroad as a brakeman for the last several years but had been an amateur wrestler prior to that. The two had met after she went to work in the dispatch office and now here we sat.

I tried to study him without being obvious. He seemed nice enough but not too bright with a dull personality and was definitely more interested in cleaning his plate than carrying on a conversation. But conversation wasn't necessary anyway. Nadine kept up prattle of useless banter punctuated with nervous laughter causing other diners to turn and look in our direction.

It was an uncomfortable hour and I was relieved when she announced that we were through with lunch and would be moving on to the next phase of this terribly awkward day.

Together in the hotel where she had rented a room she scolded me for not being more appropriately dressed for her occasion. I had worn a pleated skirt, white blouse and a tailored jacket and had not brought a change of clothes. "I'm surprised you didn't wear your Sloppy Joe sweater and Bobby Sox." She scoffed. I let the remark pass. Surely this day would eventually come to an end.

The office of the Justice of The Peace consisted of a scarred wooden desk located in the corner of the living room of his home. A small framed plaque certifying that he indeed was the Town Magistrate and thereby authorized to perform such ceremonies hung on the wall behind his desk.

Jim and a friend who would serve as his witness arrived shortly after we did and in a matter of minutes the ceremony was performed, marriage certificate witnessed and signed and I found myself being hustled off to the station to await the arrival of the bus for the trip back to the University.

With the whirlwind activities of the day behind me, I sat and reflected on the day's events. Where was the romance which I had supposed would accompany weddings? Could one really call this a wedding? What on earth did these two people have in common?

But I turned my concerns and empathy to Jim. Poor, unsuspecting fellow. He could not possibly have guessed that he had unwittingly pushed open the door to his own private Armageddon. But then again, he was an experienced wrestler. Maybe he could take her down.

As if climaxing the somberness of a wasted day, a cold October rain began to fall splashing giant drops of wet exclamation points against the windshield as the bus rumbled through the early evening hours on the way back to the University.

By the time I arrived back on campus it was too late to participate in Homecoming opening ceremonies.

FRANCIS'S FOLLY

Francis Long and I were probably two of the most unlikely individuals on campus to form a friendship. We had absolutely nothing in common. She was an only child in what appeared to be an affluent family. I never knew for sure what her father's occupation was but assumed he was a rancher.

I had spent a weekend or two with her at her home north of Santa Fe where she and her parents lived in a rambling, ranch type house furnished with Southwestern décor. Each time I visited there were a large number of noisy people in the house. There was a party atmosphere and an abundance of food and alcohol being served. I wasn't sure if this was a typical life style for them or just weekend happenings, but it was a foreign lifestyle for me and I was uncomfortable there.

Francis did not share a room in the dorm. Her unmade bed was usually piled with clothes, empty shopping bags and senseless odds and ends that didn't seem to belong anywhere and she seldom passed room inspection.

She viewed the House Mothers in the same light as prison inmates do Wardens and believed the rules were made for someone other than herself. Although she was constantly confined to campus for one infraction or another she managed to sneak by the 'guards' and attend most of the social functions. She smuggled beer into her room, lit one cigarette off the other and unknown to me at the time, harbored a disturbing secret.

She was a sophomore also and a music major. Her chain smoking didn't seem to have had an adverse effect on her voice, a lovely contralto, and she was talented enough to play her own piano accompaniment at her recitals.

The two of us were on the intramural basketball team where she played guard position. She could rough up an opposing player just enough to make you glad you didn't play on their team.

I think what I found attractive about her in an odd way was her sheer spunkiness rather than one of being a kindred spirit.

Never one to be hampered by protocol, she walked into my room unexpectedly one Saturday afternoon and sprawled across my bed shoes and all.

"How much money do you have?" she asked as she lit a cigarette.

I had managed to put aside around fifty dollars from the small allowance from home and the earnings from my job on campus.

"Why?" I wanted to know.

"Rosenthals is having a sale. I want a new coat and God knows you need one. Get your nose out of that book and let's go see what they've got."

She was right about my coat. I had owned it since high school and it had become a little worn and I didn't mind taking a break from the books for a while.

We tried on several coats and finally decided on identical ones except in different colors. I was pleased that I was able to purchase a pretty, warm, all-weather coat and still have a little money left over.

We paid for our purchases and walked back to the dorm.

Back in my room, she tried on her coat again. "How does this look?' she wanted to know as she flung a knitted scarf around her neck and pulled on a pair of matching gloves.

"Where did those come from?" I asked.

"They were on that table by the front door. Didn't you see them?"

As a matter of fact, I hadn't seen them. Nor had I seen the clerk ring them up when we paid for our purchases.

I finished hanging my coat in the closet.

"Hey", I said. "I've got to get this report finished. I'll see you at the gym tomorrow. Ok?"

"Sure. See ya." She walked out of the room still wearing her coat, scarf, and gloves. She seemed oblivious to my not so subtle brush off but I wasn't able to shake a nagging feeling of uneasiness that I couldn't quite put my finger on as I returned to my books.

This was the first time but would not be the last that I would be embarrassed by Francis' uncontrollable compulsion.

"I want you to take a walk with me." She said one evening a few weeks later as we dried off in the locker room shower after a basketball game. "I want you to see something."

"What is it?" I wanted to know.

"Just do it." She urged. "We have time before we have to report back to our cells."

We pulled on our jeans and sweaters and walked the few blocks to Sixth Street. She made a quick turn here and kept walking. We stopped in front of a white two story frame house."

"Well, what do you think?" She asked grinding out her second cigarette on the front walk.

"Francis? Of what?" Stop the mystery.

"The woman who owns this place rents rooms and apartments to college kids. And she has a vacancy right now. I've already checked it out."

"So what's that got to do with us?'

"Look". She turned to me, "Those old Biddies at the dorm are driving me nuts. They're on my case all the time. I can't make a move that they don't know about it. I think they have been snooping through my things. We can rent this place, share expenses and save money besides. You can have the bedroom and I'll take the couch in the living room. Come on, let's get out of that damned dorm," she pleaded.

Actually, I didn't have a problem with being in the dorm but coincidentally, I had just received a letter from Dad telling me that I might not be able to finish the year. The reason, of course, was finances. Nadine and Jim were having marital problems (was anyone surprised) and she needed help again.

Seeing this as a possible solution to both our problems, I agreed and that weekend with the help of some of the fellows that owned a car, we moved into the small, upstairs utility apartment.

"I hope you know how to cook," I said as I took inventory of the modest supply of utensils in the kitchen. In an effort to 'stay out of their way', I had spent more time outdoors than inside while I was living at home and being in the kitchen was unfamiliar to me.

"Enough to get by."

We soon had the place set up and although it lacked anything that could be considered out of the ordinary as far as décor was concerned, I had to admit that it was more hospitable than the dorm rooms.

We made a list of the few housekeeping items we would need and decided to go shopping at Kress Variety Store the following day.

Inside the store we split up. We had decided that she would shop for kitchen items while I took care of toiletries. Later we would shop for food together. I was grateful, again, that I had saved enough money to hold up my end of the arrangement.

We paid for our purchases at separate registers and as we walked toward the front of the store she said, "I'll meet you at the door. I saw something I want to check out for next time."

I waited near the door until she appeared from behind one of the counters.

"Ok, I'm ready," she said as we reached the door.

"Not so fast, Ladies." We were stopped by the sound of a deep voice and a large hand clamped over our shoulders.

I looked up into the angry face of the store manager.

"I need to see you in my office," he directed us with a jerk of his head.

Startled and surprised, I looked at Francis. Her face was expressionless and showed virtually no emotion as he guided us toward his office while keeping a firm grip on our shoulders.

Once inside his office he ordered us to sit in chairs opposite his desk.

"Give me your bag. Let me see your receipt." His eyes bore into me. Obediently, I produced both, placing the bag on his desk. He only glanced at the items and receipt before handing them back to me then turned to Francis.

"You too", he demanded.

She hesitantly placed the bag on his desk.

"And the receipt." He was livid with anger and very nearly snatched the paper from her hand.

As he read each item on the receipt, he removed the matching merchandise from the bag and lined them up across his large desk. "And where is your receipt for these?" He held up a plastic napkin holder and a cheap set of salt and pepper shakers.

Without waiting for her response, he leaned across the desk and looked directly into her eyes, "You have been in here before". He was having difficulty controlling his anger. "I've never stopped you until now, but hear this, if I see either of you in here again, I'll call the Cops as well as the Dean of the University. Now get the hell out of my store."

He tossed the items she had paid for back in her bag and yanked the door open.

"Get out"! He repeated.

Outside on the street, I turned to Francis. Humiliated and furious, I pounded on her arm. "Damn you Francis. You could have gotten us in serious trouble. If my dad hears about this, he'll jerk me out of school for sure." I continued to vent my anger. "We didn't even need that stuff and anyway, you had enough money to pay for it. Why did you do that"?

I realized I was becoming shrill and probably attracting attention from inside the store. I stopped shouting and took a moment to catch my breath. She had remained perfectly quiet not even reacting to my pounding.

I looked at her face and for the first time since I had known her saw through her tough veneer. Tears were welling up in her eyes. "Because—they were there", she answered haltingly.

We walked the rest of the way to the rooming house in silence and I don't recall that the subject ever came up again but I considered this to be a lesson in Trust 101 and vowed to never go shopping with Francis Long again.

OUT-OF-THEIR-WAY

Three days each week the girls basketball team had a practice session after dinner that lasted an hour or longer. By the time we showered and changed clothes it was usually near dark.

Francis and I walked directly to the apartment on those days rather than taking a detour to the library.

As we turned up the walkway one evening, she nudged me and said, "I wonder who that guy is that always walks behind us."

"Who do you mean?" I wanted to know.

"Don't you pay attention to anything? He walks a little distance behind us and when we turn in here, he keeps walking up the street."

"No, I haven't noticed, Francis. Who cares?"

The fact was I was becoming increasingly irritated with her. The incident at the store had obviously had more of an impact on me than it had on her. There was still an indication that she hadn't changed her ways but merely the location which she pilfered from. A silly plastic toy train had appeared on the book shelf and was increasing in length one car at a time. In addition, a sugar dispenser obviously taken from a restaurant had suddenly appeared on our kitchen table.

Moving to the apartment with her had been beneficial in that I was able to deal with my strapped finances more easily but I was questioning the wisdom of my decision. I didn't view her problem in the light of the illness that it apparently was, but rather as a reckless and childish lack of respect for rules and authority.

I was becoming more and more discouraged by the fact that I would not be able to finish the two remaining years of college. This would be my last year. Student loans available through the G. I. Bill were being offered to returning service men but I knew of no way of obtaining financing for myself.

On the other hand going back home was not an option. I had come this far in my quest to find "Out-Of-Their-Way" and the thought of going back was depressing.

More and more often I felt myself falling into an emotional slump and Francis' seemingly shallow attitude toward everything was aggravating.

She had been dating a non-student whom she referred to as Mac, short for his last name MacNamara.   He ironically was the son of the town Chief of Police. I had met him and he struck me as being quiet and reserved.

One Friday as we walked to the apartment after ball practice, she turned and said, "Listen. You've been moping around for days. Mac has a friend he wants you to meet. They can pick us up tomorrow and we can all go dancing-get you out of the doldrums."

The thought of a blind date didn't appeal to me, but dancing did and considering my low state of mind I didn't see what I had to lose , so I agreed.

I was impressed with my date's excellent manners. He had an exceptionally nice voice and a friendly personality.

As the waiter cleared the table, Francis indicated we needed a break and we went to the Ladies Room. Once inside she asked, "You know who your date is, don't you?"

"What do you mean?" I wanted to know.

"He's the guy that has been following behind us all this time," she said. "Don't you recognize him?"

I didn't, but that's how I met Harold Jaffa, the young man I would marry exactly one year later.

He and I continued dating without always teaming up with Francis and Mac and one day he took me to meet his parents. He still lived at home and, as it turned out, their house was only a few houses further up the same street as our apartment.

His father had been a mining engineer in his younger days but now worked as an accountant at one of the large wholesale companies in town, and was in failing health.

He never really saw me as being acceptable in their lives and usually referred to me as 'That Girl'. Mrs. Jaffa was distantly friendly but I realized, too late, that Harold would never outgrow his 'little boy' relationship with her and I saw no indication throughout the years that she encouraged otherwise.

Mr. and Mrs. Jaffa had come from families that had migrated to America from

Germany in the early 1800's. They were distant cousins and had the same sir name so it's difficult to separate the genealogy, but according to a book by author Marc Simmons, "-two brothers, Samuel and Henry N. Jaffa came to the Southwest in pre-railroad days and shared in the general prosperity that followed."

Henry Jaffa, Mrs. Jaffa's father, was elected first Mayor of Albuquerque in 1885 and again from Mr. Simmons book, "he was hand in glove with the tight co-terie of men who occupied the town's topmost rung on the economic and social ladder."

He later broadened his politics and was elected to the office of Secretary of the Territory, the last such office prior to New Mexico's entry into statehood in 1912.

I knew nothing of this history at the time I became engaged to Harold and it wouldn't have mattered anyway, nor could I have known that as time went by, I would be made to feel more and more like "That Girl".

That summer after school was over, I took Harold to meet my family and I was relieved to see that Dad approved of him. There was no reason why he shouldn't have. But back home after a later visit to meet his family, Dad asked, "How are you going to like being married to those parents?"

"I'm not marrying them." I shot back.

"Yes," he said. "You are."

As in the past, Dad's foresight proved to be prophetically correct.

At the time I really believed that I was in love, even knowing so little about what love was. In retrospect, maybe subconsciously, I agreed to marry for the wrong reason.   But there was a wholesome innocence about our relationship that can only be captured one time in life.

We set the date for the wedding to be November 12th the anniversary of our first date and communicated regularly throughout the summer.

That fall I selected my wedding gown, a beautiful ivory satin floor length dress accented with tiny seed pearls and lace.

Relatively speaking it was a small wedding attended by our friends and close relatives. My best friend from high school was the Maid of Honor. Junior was the Ring Bearer and the only one in the wedding party that caused me any anxiety. He was only ten years old and one of the neighbors who enjoyed teasing him had told him repeatedly that by merely walking down the aisle with her, he would be marrying the Flower Girl.

I half expected him to bolt from the church, ring, pillow and all, but I under-estimated him and the two of them walked primly ahead of us dressed as a miniature Bride and Groom.

I thought Dad looked handsome as we walked down the aisle together but I couldn't miss noticing that Harold's mother was unable to restrain her sobs. His Uncle laughing told me some time later that a day or two after the wedding she had called him and tearfully asked, "I wonder what my baby is doing now?" to which he reportedly replied, "Well, Eleanor, what in hell would you expect him to be doing now?" She burst into sobs.

We rented a tiny efficiency apartment in Santa Fe and he commuted to and from work in Los Alamos where he was employed as an electrician with a construction contractor.

We were two kids playing house. I put my dreams of having a writing career behind me with absolutely no regret and replaced it with one of becoming a good wife and hopefully a mother someday.

At least twice a week Mrs. Jaffa called to check on 'her baby' and report on his father's health which according to her was rapidly declining and she was fearful of being alone if "something happened."

We went back to Las Vegas almost every weekend in order that Harold could take care of different little chores that his dad could no longer manage and to bolster his mother's spirits. On each visit meals were prepared with Harold's favorite dishes in mind. His father had quit work and only left the house to keep his appointments with his doctor. Otherwise, except for meals, he sat in his large leather chair dressed in his robe and slippers and smoked unfiltered cigarettes.

Why I didn't have the foresight to predict the inevitable seems ludicrous to me now. It's possible that my illusion of having finally reached Out-Of-Their-Way overrode my ability to see the situation facing us with celerity. But I certainly was not prepared for the ultimatum which we were informed of as a result of a family meeting that was convened a few months before our second anniversary.

Mr. Jaffa had had a mild heart attack and was confined to bed requiring constant care. We had helped move them from their two-story family home to a smaller apartment several months earlier but even that was not conducive to helping Mrs. Jaffa cope with all she had to face caring for a "self-made invalid" as Dad put it.

The only solution to the dilemma, we were told, was that they give up their apartment and move in with us.

The fact that we also lived in a small apartment and that I was now expecting our first baby in a few months didn't seem to be an issue with anyone but me and my input wasn't solicited. So instead of speaking out as I should have, I didn't object when Harold agreed to this arrangement. We were told that we were 'good children' and sent on our way.

Good children, indeed.

Within a matter of weeks his parents had disposed of most of their household goods and moved into our apartment taking the bedroom while we took the couch in the living room. Mrs. Jaffa immediately put herself in charge of the kitchen while he claimed the only easy chair in the living room.

Like pawns in a game of chess we found ourselves relegated to the position of adult children living with their parents instead of the reverse. This arrangement seemed to be a satisfactory one with Harold.

He left for work early in the morning and returned late in the evening. His time after dinner was spent playing cribbage with his father until the old man would complain of chest pains and was put to bed. Then he and his mother sat and visited until she turned in for the night. There was very little time left for the two of us to be alone.

I used my time during the day hand sewing a layette for our baby, taking walks around the neighborhood and counting down the weeks until I would become a Mother.

I missed having someone to talk to but I told myself that the loneliness that stalked me like a shadow would soon be replaced by the much anticipated arrival of this baby. I seldom heard from my own family and there didn't seem to be anyone in the vicinity of the apartment complex that was near my age with whom to develop a friendship.

Then one afternoon, like the Joker popping up in a deck of crazy playing cards, I received a phone call from Francis Long. She was in town to shop for a fall wardrobe for college and invited me to join her.

I jumped at the chance to spend time with an old acquaintance near my age and agreed to meet her at one of the high end dress shops on the Plaza.

As I followed her through the store, I watched her push through rack after rack of clothing, selecting sweaters, blouses and skirts with no apparent concern as to the tab she was running up.

Finally, satisfied with, "That will do for a starter," she carried the armload of hangers to the register and paid the clerk with large bills.

We passed a table of leather gloves marked with a sale price of two dollars a pair. Without a moment's hesitation she slipped a pair into her huge shopping bag and we out of the store.

Francis dropped me off at the apartment and I lapsed into a moment of nostalgia as I watched her drive away. I felt a sense of regret for not having been able to complete my college education. Harold's long hours at work and the financial burden of caring for his parents was a sobering issue. The responsibilities that had been thrust onto our young marriage had taken some of the youthfulness out of our lives.

Though the opposite was true, suddenly I felt years older than Francis. She still maintained a reckless, audacious attitude toward life-always the free spirited, unfettered person with little or no responsibilities.

The baby stirring in my womb broke my moment of reflection and I rechanneled my thoughts to my own situation. Being a wife and mother was my calling. One I had dreamed of since childhood while playing with my dolls.

I waved to her as she rounded the corner at the end of the block and whispered into space, "Goodbye, old friend. I wouldn't change places with you for all the world."

That was the last time I saw Francis. I have no idea what became of her but I hope she eventually recognized her problem and got some professional help. Otherwise I visualize her these many years later as a stooped, shriveled, old woman taking napkin holders and odds and ends of silverware from the dining table and stealthily tucking them under her mattress in some nursing home somewhere.

JANUARY 1950

Construction work had tapered off at Los Alamos during the winter months of 1949 and Harold was able to work shorter hours and be home on the weekends.

This meant that we had less money coming in but I was grateful to have the extra time with him. My pregnancy had been a difficult one. I would gain a few pounds only to find out during the next doctor's appointment that I had lost the gain and a pound or two more. Nausea was a prevailing problem throughout the entire eight and half months and was not restricted to 'morning sickness' exclusively. The mere scent of food cooking or the odor of soap in the detergent section of the grocery store would send me frantically searching for the restroom.

So I found it comforting to have Harold home to lean on and to discuss my apprehensions with. I had broached some of my pregnancy concerns with Mrs. Jaffa only to be deluged with Old Wives tales interlaced with superstitions.

We spent our time together now taking long walks, considering names, speculating whether we wanted a boy or girl and always concluding that it didn't really matter either way.

One night each week his parents and we would spend playing Canasta with Harold's Uncle Ben and his wife, Sally. They also lived in Santa Fe and owned a lovely home, beautifully furnished and equipped with the most modern conveniences. They owned a gourmet restaurant just off the Plaza which was renowned for its distinctive menu.

Ben was a tall, handsome, heavy-set, balding man with a well groomed moustache, large brown eyes and a wonderful sense of humor.

Sally had grown up in an orphanage along with her younger sister, Aurora who lived with them. They were both registered nurses and had been two of the most frequently requested caregivers whenever a family needed private duty nurses in their homes. Sally had resigned from nursing when she married Ben and after several miscarriages had given birth to their only child, Joe. He was a spoiled, totally undisciplined four year old when I first met him.

These evenings were spent sitting around their long dining table with cocktails, snacks and a room shrouded in a blue haze from our cigarette smoke. It is astonishing how ignorant we were then regarding the harmful effects of smoking or even worse, inhaling second-hand smoke. But there we sat on the evening of January 1, 1950 when I began to feel my first labor pains.

We drove Harold's parents back to the apartment, picked up the small suitcase I had packed in advance and with a feeling of eager anticipation we drove to St. Vincent Hospital several blocks away.

Aurora had preceded us to the hospital and was waiting for as we checked in at the admission desk. She hurried me down the hall toward the maternity section leaving Harold staring after us in bewilderment.

Within minutes she had me undressed, wrapped in a hospital gown, strapped to a gurney and with the help of an aid was rolling me down a long hall.

Large doors swung open and I found myself trying to shield my eyes from the blinding brightness of the large overhead light as strong hands lifted me onto the delivery table. I had never before felt such fright mixed with anticipation. I turned to survey my surroundings and saw the doctor donning his green scrubs with the assistance of a nurse. He crossed the room to the side of the table, slowly moved his cold stethoscope over my abdomen several times listening intently then spoke urgently to the nurse standing at the head of the table. "Put her under."

A heavy hand pressed the rubber mask over my face and I felt the heady effects of inhaling the pungent odor of ether being forced into my nostrils.

For an interminable time, it seemed, I drifted in an abyss of darkness. In my semi-conscious state I tumbled like a leaf in the wind helplessly trying to grasp hold of anything that would stop the downward spiraling and allow me to catch hold of something that would bring me back to that bright light that had been my last recollection of reality.

Gradually the spinning slowed. Voices sounding as though they were spoken from an echo chamber became audible. But at the same time a strangely ominous silence pervaded the room. I listened intently.

It was the heart wrenching absence of a newborn baby's cry.

I realized that my eyes were covered with a large damp cloth and struggled to remove it but found that my hands were restrained at the wrists. Panic gripped me and I cried out. "Where's my baby?"

Silence.

I called for Aurora. Surely she would have stayed nearby.

Silence.

The quiet voice of Doctor Ward was speaking now as one of the nurses released the restraints holding my ankles and wrists. "Anita", gently, "there was a problem. Your baby is dead. She was stillborn."

She. A girl. Dead. I pulled the thin sheet that was covering me over my face, curled into a fetal position and wept uncontrollably.

"Poor Harold", I sobbed. I knew he had his heart set on having a daughter.

It was January 2, 1950.

GRIEF ABATED

I have no recollection of how long I was kept hospitalized.

Harold and his mother selected a white and pink batiste dress I had embroidered from the layette, chose the cemetery lot as well as the tiny white casket and arranged for a simple burial ceremony conducted by a local Rabbi.

Back at the apartment, I packed away the layette; tortured myself with guilt, wondering what I had done or failed to do that could have caused this unexpected and unexplained tragedy in our lives, and along with Harold, lapsed into a gulf of depression.

The two of us seemed to wander aimlessly in a wilderness of grief and disappointment. But within a few days he returned to work and I resumed my lonely walks. Only now instead of walking the familiar streets of the neighborhood, I extended my range and visited the cemetery.

I sat near the tiny plot of still raised earth and ran my hand over the engraving on the small white headstone:

BABY GIRL JAFFA

JANUARY 2 1950

No name, though we had chosen one. Just twenty five strokes of a stone cutters chisel signifying a life that never lived.

I desperately needed the comfort and condolence usually found in the confines of one's biological family and I considered contacting the folks to see if I could come home for a few days but Nadine had recently left her eighteen month old baby in Mother's care while she was off engaged in another of her wayward pursuits so I abandoned the idea and withdrew even more unto myself.

As the months went by, Mr. Jaffa's health continued to decline. He had been admitted to the hospital several times for emergency treatment, required numerous house calls by his heart specialist and was now dependent on in-home oxygen to relieve the stress of breathing when he was having an attack.

Ludicrous as this all seems knowing what we do today, he still managed to shuffle out to the front porch in his robe and slippers to inhale a few puffs from a cigarette believing he was taking in less nicotine by cutting it in half.

The months dragged slowly and mournfully by. Mrs. Jaffa devoted all of her time to caring for her husband and was near exhaustion herself but continued to insist on maintaining her reign over the kitchen which suited me well. I hadn't really ever learned to cook and besides I had recently begun experiencing the now familiar symptoms of early pregnancy nausea.

But this time rather than spending my time in eager anticipation, my days were clouded with anxiety fueled by Mrs. Jaffa's repeated renditions of how the likelihood of giving birth to a live baby after having a stillborn child was marginal at best.

So it was with a keen sense of foreboding that I found myself being wheeled through the familiar swinging double doors of the delivery room at St. Vincent's a mere thirteen months and few weeks later.

Linda's arrival in the early morning hours on February 20th left no doubt with anyone within hearing range that I had given birth to a baby that was very much alive.

Weighing considerably less than six pounds, with tiny fists clinched and pummeling the air, mouth wide-open protesting having been evicted from the warm amniotic sac she had been floating in for nine months and being slapped on the naked bottom by old Doctor Ward's gloved hand, she loudly announced her arrival into a cold, stark world.

She was quickly swaddled in soft warm blankets, placed in the curve of my arm and an ecstatic Mother and a snip of a baby, still raising hell, were wheeled to the maternity ward, moved from the gurney and onto our bed where we both fell asleep completely exhausted from our individual efforts.

CHANGED LIVES

"Well, your life will never be the same." Doctor Lathrop remarked as he finished his post natal exam in preparation to discharging us from the hospital. "Babies have a way of changing things in ways we don't anticipate. Call the office for an appointment in about six weeks and we'll see how things are going. Good luck." He shook my hand, gave Linda a tender stroke on the cheek and left us to be wheeled down the hall to the elevator by the nurse who had just entered the room.

Bundled in soft new blankets to protect her from a wet February snow, Linda made her first appearance into the outside world and her introduction to her grandmother and grandfather Jaffa who welcomed her enthusiastically.

The doctor had not spoken in jest. Our routine lives were quickly transformed into one of mixing formulas, sterilizing bottles, boiling water washing load after load of baby gowns, blankets and diapers which needed (we believed then) to be boiled. Everything, it seemed, needed to be sterilized and boiled (new mothers who had had a difficult delivery had suggested that fathers be included) before they touched a newborn baby.

Ten o'clock feedings, Two a.m. feedings and round after round of rocking a colicky baby filled our days and many nights. Nevertheless, it was an exciting time for all of us. Even Mr. Jaffa's spirits seemed to improve and he spent less time in bed and more in the room where the baby was.

Linda was a beautiful baby with big blue eyes and golden hair that curled in ringlets. She thrived on attention and good care and overnight it seems became a precocious, inquisitive toddler full of mischief and energy.

But outside the focus of this new phase of our life, things were beginning to take a downward spiral. The government contract at Los Alamos was in the final stages of completion meaning that Harold's job would be coming to an end as well.   Additionally, Mr. Jaffa's health took a serious turn for the worse. Early in the evening on November 22, 1952 He suffered a severe heart attack. He was rushed to the hospital where he passed away later that night.

Recognizing the need for more living space, we had moved from the small apartment into a three bedroom house before Linda was born. Now the hospital bills, funeral expenses and loss of a well-paying job put a strain on our resources and marriage. We found a smaller house for rent that was more in line with our finances and moved there but construction work in general had slacked off during the winter months and we still struggled to make ends meet.

Mrs. Jaffa was almost inconsolable. Her comfort seemed to be derived from doting on Linda and increasing her dependency on Harold.

As our financial situation continued to decline, I realized that I had no alternative but to go to work myself. I applied for a job at the Telephone Company and was hired as a long distance operator. As it turned out, this would be the beginning of a long and rewarding career with the company but at that particular time I was reluctant and even resentful of the need to leave Linda even though I knew her grandmother would give her the best of care.

Eventually the stagnant job market began to turn around and Harold returned to work. Only now the job was in the uranium mines located outside the small town of Grants over one hundred miles away. Daily commuting was out of the question. This meant that he would arrive home late in the evening on Friday and leave on Sunday afternoon. Often inclement weather prevented him from coming home at all. As time went by, this arrangement became more and more exacting and unsatisfactory.

Gradually the housing industry began experiencing a building boom in the post war era and the government was offering low interest loans with no down payments to Veterans on the G.I. Bill.

Harold qualified for a loan and we decided to buy a house in Albuquerque in a new subdivision that was being developed. Not only would we be cutting his commute time almost in half allowing him to spend more time at home with us, but we would be purchasing our first home.

The four of us relocated to Albuquerque in 1955 and began a new life although a somewhat apprehensive one. The total cost of the house was ten thousand dollars with monthly payments of seventy-five dollars which seemed like a staggering amount at that time. But Harold's job paid well and appeared to be long term.

I resigned from the Telephone Company and set about decorating and furnishing our first home.

Mike was born the following year and I'm positive that he was born smiling. I do not own one childhood photograph of him that does not picture him with a broad and sometimes toothless smile. Even today as a middle-aged hulk of a man, it is unusual to find him unsmiling or in an unpleasant mood.

Union strikes and temporary lay-offs again plagued our resources and I returned to work again.

But our marriage now began to suffer. Like a plant neglected from lack of sunshine and water, we failed to nurture our relationship and eventually like the unattended plant, it withered and died.

Twelve years after finally reaching the elusive "Out-Of-Thelr-Way", our marriage ended in divorce.

A TOUGH ROW TO HOE

Following the divorce, Harold sold the house and he and his mother rented an apartment in a complex and I found an older house to rent that was run down, badly in need of paint, owned by a heartless landlord and altogether equal to the circumstances that I found myself in.

With the help of a girl friend who had survived a similar situation we bought a few gallons of paint, painted the interior, scrubbed the cabinets, bathroom and floors and hung some pretty curtains over the windows. In a few days we had transformed the house into a cheerful place to live.

The move necessitated placing Linda and Mike in a Day Care which was located several blocks away as was the school where Linda would attend second grade.

Although we had owned two cars, Harold insisted on keeping them both so each morning we were up at the crack of dawn, ate our breakfast which usually consisted of hot oatmeal, toast and milk and then, because the Day Care was too far for the children to walk, I bundled them in a heavy quilt, loaded them into their toy wagon and pulled them down the busy street to Smart Day Nursery. I saw them safely inside then waited to catch the downtown bus to go to work.

It was with a heavy heart and many distractions in my mind that I managed my work day. Thoughts of Linda walking alone to and from a new school in an unfamiliar neighborhood tormented my mind. Mike had become very attached to his grandmother and though he seldom complained, I knew he hated the day care. He would tearfully cling to me when I left each morning and again to Linda when she left for school.

Although Harold seldom paid the child support ordered in the divorce decree, he still was entitled to visitation rights and I never discouraged them. Both Linda and Mike were emotionally attached to their grandmother and to him and the divorce had been upsetting for us all.

My salary wasn't sufficient enough to allow for anything but the bare necessities and he and his mother were able to provide them with a more carefree lifestyle that all children are entitled to.

They spent much of the summer with their dad and grandmother. She treated them to Elvis Pressley movies and trips to the zoo. They were loaded with gifts at Christmas time and spent a great vacation at Sea World that first summer. Under the circumstances, I didn't see these indulgences as being anything more than what they deserved.

Over time and with determined perseverance I learned to manage my resources and time more efficiently and we moved to a small, neat two bedroom house with a yard large enough to accommodate a swing set and sand box. We adopted a pound puppy named Murphy and settled into a more normal routine.

In between my two terms of employment at the phone company, I had worked for three years at the power company as an audit clerk. My duties there consisted of estimating meter usage on customer accounts when the Meter Reader was unable to gain access to the meter for an actual reading. I took the previous three months readings, calculated an average consumption of usage and marked the meter card with a Mark Sense pencil that could be translated through a computer process for billing.

The person in charge of the computer operation was a young, handsome Italian man with coal black hair and eyes and a wonderful smile by the name of Ed. He was divorced with a young daughter and had been employed with the company since shortly after being discharged from the Army Air Force in 1948.

Our jobs interfaced in as much as the meter cards that I had marked needed to be scheduled through his computer operations then returned to me to be filed manually.

"You are new here, aren't you?' He had asked the first time I took the cards to be processed.

"Yes, and frankly, I'm a little intimidated by this entire procedure. We did everything manually or with posting machines where I worked before."

"Well intimidation doesn't sit very well here," he grinned. "Come on. I'll give you the VIP tour while your cards are 'cooking'." He showed me around the department, introducing me to the other computer operators and the keypunch clerks. When he had finished he handed my cards back to me.

"Next is the coffee shop. Have you had your break yet?"

When I said I hadn't, "Let's go. The coffee shop is upstairs."

That began a friendship that lasted throughout my employment there. Just coffee,, or sometimes sitting together for lunch or walking around the block to finish a break. He was always the first to greet me in the mornings and walked me to the bus at the end of the day and I found myself looking forward to the next day just because of these small gestures of thoughtfulness and kindness.

GETTING IT RIGHT

I'm not exactly sure when I fell in love with Ed Rozzi.

We never saw each other outside the office. He was recently divorced and still "leaning back". I had been divorced for a longer period of time but I wasn't comfortable leaving Linda and Mike in the evenings and definitely not inclined to bring someone new into their lives.

But when I left that company to return to work at the Telephone Company, I received phone calls from him there which over time led to a quick snack or drink after work before I had to catch the bus and pick up the kids at Day Care.

Five years after our first very casual meeting and by now having become best friends, Eddie and I were married.

This was the start of the longest most fulfilling time I ever expect to know in this lifetime.

For the first time I understood that 'happy' was more than a word. It was an emotion of the soul.

Our early years of marriage were spent with the variegated trials of adjusting to our new life with each other and our children and finding boundaries between the 'your' and 'my' syndrome. Both sets of kids were awkward with having a step parent so we never insisted that they refer to us by anything but our first names.

We worked hard, dreamed big and spent our times alone planning and saving toward building our dream home.

Jim was born in 1963 six weeks earlier than expected and the only time until he was in his early forties that that particular phenomena occurred in his timing. His internal clock always seemed to be behind or in need of being rewound. We nicknamed him "The Governor", later shortened to 'Gov' due to his odd way of crying in strange little broken sentences of starts and stops, as if trying to make a speech. From toddler to the present time his sense of humor and flair for mimicry has kept the family gatherings roaring with laughter.

In 1965 Harold secured an extremely high salaried job with a construction company that had a long term government contract repairing damaged air strips caused by the war in Viet Nam and left the United States. His leaving upset Mike's and Linda's life in ways that he surely could not have anticipated at the time.

Mrs. Jaffa, who until now, had been immovable in her belief that she could not bear to be alone found herself in just that situation and was in deep grief. I was highly resentful that in his apparent quest for big money he would not recognize the disruption and upheaval that his departure was causing in the lives of those he was leaving behind.

But leave he did. He rarely communicated with his children and with only one exception, when he returned to the States to attend his mother's funeral, he never came back.

He met and married a Thai woman when the company he worked for relocated to Bangkok. They had two small children and from all indications he adopted that countries customs and lifestyle as his own.

We received word that he had died there in the early '90's and is buried somewhere in that land.

THE GOLDEN YEARS

With the inevitable passage of time we moved on with our lives.

Having tenure and a dedicated work ethic, both Eddie and I were rewarded with advancement and increased earnings by our employers and we built our dream home in 1972. It was a beautiful tri-level on a one –third acre lot in an upscale neighborhood. We added a swimming pool and installed landscaping. Gradually we furnished it in our chosen décor and started an extensive art collection.

The frustrating aspect for me was that the top soil had been removed when the house was being constructed leaving the remaining soil of such poor quality that no matter how diligently I worked, I could not coax the daisies I had planted in the flower beds to mature and bloom.

Realizing my disappointment that my favorite flower was not likely to have much success thriving in the poor soil, Eddie laughed at my frustration but made it a point to bring back a bouquet of fresh cut daisies almost every time he returned from a shopping errand. This little touch of tenderness became a ritual over the years and recalling those special times now bring back bittersweet memories.

We watched our children develop from childhood to adolescence; attended school plays, Boy Scout and ROTC meetings, Spelling Bee competitions and sports events. We cheered at Pine Wood Derby races and track meets. We applauded their successes and attempted to make light of their failures and youthful mistakes.

One by one we watched them reach adulthood, choose their life's partners and begin lives in a world apart from ours.

Linda was the first to leave. She was seventeen and though mature for her years, in her mind at least, much too young to marry.

She had met a young man who had been born in Germany and was a relatively new citizen of the United States. He had recently joined the Navy and was soon to leave for boot camp in San Diego. It quickly became apparent that with or without our sanction, she was determined to skip her last year of high school and marry Harold Woods , who was not much older than she.

We arranged a simple but lovely wedding with my dad giving her away and their closest friends and both families attending.

Choking back lumps in our throats we watched them drive away in an ancient Nash Rambler they had purchased for almost nothing. As they drove out of sight ahead of the plume of black exhaust spewing from the little overloaded vehicle, Eddie remarked, "One by one we will watch all of them drive over that little hill and out of our lives."

He was right.

His daughter married a fellow who had recently enlisted in the Army and they too moved away. Although she had never lived with us, Eddie kept in close touch with her and he missed the personal communications and visits.

Mike married his high school sweetheart, Kristine and even though they remained in Albuquerque, they made their home in another part of the city and stayed busy with their careers and personal lives.

Only Jim remained at home and was finishing his last year in high school but was making plans to join the Navy soon after graduation. Harold had been his idol and very persuasive in making this decision.

In the meantime we were able to live our dream of travel and leisure. There was a beautiful two week vacation in Hawaii, a Caribbean Cruise, a ten day trip enjoying a tour of Europe and two fabulous shopping trips to Hong Kong.

We purchased a thirty-six foot long RV and made numerous trips exploring interesting places inside our own country but primarily for visits to Jim and Linda and Harold all of whom were now stationed on the east coast.

Jim had married a beautiful girl but as it would turn out, a very poor choice for a mate.

Linda and Harold were now the parents of two children, Matthew and Summer and were purchasing their first home in Virginia Beach.

Mike and Kris had also become parents of two children Kelly and Kyle and purchasing a beautiful home as well.

Jim and Lisa and their two children, Ryan and Megan did not fare as well. Their marriage failed and Jim became the sole parent to raise their children with virtually no moral or financial support from their mother.

True to Eddie's predictions, we watched our families grow, leave home, become parents themselves and begin a life on their own.

We retired from our careers a few years apart and were freed from the work routine enabling us to do more traveling and sightseeing.

While visiting the east coast we had become particularly attracted to a place in the Chesapeake Bay area. Near the Bay Bridge there was a wonderful parking area which allowed us to park and walk back to an overlook on the bridge.

With no way to know that this would be our last there, we made a trip in 1987 and parked on the now familiar site.

We each chose a small pebble, tossed it into the water and watched the water percolate in protest of this invasion. Two tiny circles emerged, expanded, embraced, became one then disappeared.

"In relation to the entire universe," Eddie said philosophically, "I suppose we humans are a lot like those stones. We enter our world, make one splash at best, reach out hopeful of drawing others to us, but then we leave never knowing what impact our circle may have made."

Should I have had a response to that I wondered? I wasn't sure. These musings and observations were a new phase of his personality that had begun to surface and often left me with no words with which to reply.

We sat dangling our legs from the pier tossing chunks of bread left from our lunch to greedy gulls and watched the sun set.

Sky and water converge in a blaze of brilliant fires and liquid gold, illuminating the horizon. The tiny peaks of sails on distant ships showed their insignificance against this background.

Then suddenly the day ended. Evening drew her grey curtains across the silent drama playing out before us and we felt the chill of the nights arrival.

We pulled ourselves to our feet but lingered a while longer lost in the intensity of having witnessed together a few brief moments of nature's perfection.

We had repeated this ritual several times in the past but I felt an uneasy foreboding of finality now. And maybe he did too.

"The one who is left should keep coming back here," he said. "You know, just to remember and touch all this again."

The one who is left?

I really didn't like the somber moods that seemed to creep into his thoughts more and more often now and I was glad to return to the RV and continue out trip to visit Jim and Lisa and Ryan in Philadelphia.

A WORLD UPSIDE DOWN

Something was wrong. Very wrong.

We had decided to take a break from traveling for a while and do some refurbishing to the house.

We painted the interior and had some cabinetry built to display some of the mementos we had collected on our trips.

At the same time Eddie became increasingly dispirited and easily agitated. Always the optimist, he was beginning to become a worrier. News of the conflict in the Persian Gulf and the potential of war there was particularly upsetting and when he learned that Harold's ship, the Nassau, was being sent into the conflict he became extremely apprehensive.

His favorite past time of preparing the evening meal became more and more of a chore as days went by. I insisted in taking over in the kitchen but the smell of food cooking made him nauseated. We began eating out as much as possible but after taking a few bites he would push his plate away and pressure me to hurry with my meal so we could go home. He slept fitfully and often woke in the early hours and paced restlessly about the house.

One afternoon he insisted on driving to the cemetery where his parents were buried. The rose bushes in our yard were in full bloom and he wanted to take some there.

As we stood at the grave sites he said, almost wistfully, "I wonder who will bring us flowers?"

This show of melancholy was extremely disturbing to me. Until the past few weeks Eddie had an enviable appreciation for life. Even the simple things like washing his face in a cold mountain stream; watching flirtatious squirrels scamper through the amber leaves in Boston Common and the migration of Sand Hill Cranes and Snow Geese feeding in the Bosque.

Never are good friends appreciated more than in a time of crisis. A couple who was particularly close to us recommended we see their doctor. Overriding his protest, "I've just picked up a bug somewhere," I arranged for an appointment.

After a few preliminary tests the doctor recommended that he be admitted to the hospital for more extensive testing. Surprisingly, Eddie agreed to this and a steady procession of professionals was called into action.

Tapping, probing questioning and consulting with one another in a language decipherable only by one fluent in medical-speak, they began their work.

Titles that until now were only headings in the classified section of the telephone directory took on a personal meaning: Oncologist, Endocrinologist, Cardiologist, Rheumatologist, and others. Like a small intelligent army they gathered their data to be analyzed and researched, each of them dedicated to unraveling the mystery illness that was now rapidly ravishing his body.

I refused to leave the hospital once he had been admitted and the staff was kind enough to bring in a large leather recliner which could be converted into a daybed at night.

As the days dragged interminably by with no results from the tests, I watched Eddie's condition deteriorate before my eyes.

I hounded the doctors mercilessly for answers and action only to be assured that every prognosis was being carefully analyzed.

"I suspect Lymphoma," the doctor said as I walked down the hall with him following one of his visits. "But Ed doesn't need to know yet. We have more tests to do in order to be sure."

Precisely at that moment I understood the palpability of fear. A steel fist ripped through my chest and clamped cold fingers around my heart.

Surely the doctor was mistaken. There would have been some warning sign. Some clue.

Had there been and I had failed to recognize it?

Oh God!

More tests. Technicians tapped into his veins filling vile after vial after vial with his blood and hurried of to the lab. Liquid intake and output became a matter of statistical data. Temperature and blood pressure checks were done more and more frequently and fluctuated erratically. Additional pills were added to the tiny plastic cups.

The steel fist held me firmly In its grip.

"We're scheduling you for a bone marrow test tomorrow," the Oncology Specialist who had taken over his case said on her visit the first day. "You'll have some discomfort but we will anesthetize you and you won't remember it when you wake up."

She glanced from one of us to the other, "Do either of you have any questions?"

Yes! Why is this happening? Why has our world gone crazy? We shake our heads numbly.

Alone, we held hands and searched each other's faces. We try to read each other's emotions while struggling with our own. I saw behind his mask. He knew. Fear had claimed another captive.

DIAGNOSIS

Lymphoma.   Confirmed.

The Monster had a name. Speaking in terms she might use with a child, the doctor explained the battle that had been raging in his body.

"We can treat this," she said. "It will be tough but I believe you are up to the task. Are you with me?"

He nodded and jokingly asked, "What 's my other choice?"

Now he was whisked away to surgery. A catheter was to be implanted in his chest. His Chemotherapy would be administered through its protruding tube.

During the two hours in the surgical waiting room I flipped aimlessly through dog-eared magazines, studied the faces of my new companions and completely rearranged our lives.

No more trips. That's ok. We've seen enough.

There would be many return trips to the outpatient clinic for his treatments. That's alright. We could do it.

We would need to pace our lives. No problem. We still had life.

Back from surgery he was groggy but with lifted spirits. "We are on our way,", he smiled, weakly.

I grasped his hand, "Yes. We can make it. Don't give up," I begged.

He smiled, squeezed my fingers and fell asleep.

Even now I had borrowed some of his strength to bolster my own.

As I watched him sleep I struggled with conflicting emotions welling up inside me and tears that I dare not shed lest he awaken, solidified and lodged in my throat. I silently cursed the demon that had transformed his wonderful face into a mask of pain.

Wrapped in a blanket and sipping cold coffee from a Styrofoam cup I prepared for another nights vigil at his bedside.

Eddie's condition seemed improved, though slightly, the following morning when Kris came to visit and they both insisted I take a break from the hospital and go home for a brief rest.

The familiar streets took on a strange foreign aspect as I steered the car through the noon traffic. It occurred to me that it had been days if not weeks since I had ventured away from the hospital other than to take a brief walk around the grounds where there was a small garden.

When they came to visit, Mike and Kris had brought a change of clothing and toiletries and I had utilized the shower off the visitor's waiting room so as not to be away from the room for any length of time.

I was looking forward to a long relaxing shower in my own bathroom and maybe stretching out on the couch for a quick nap.

Even the house that we both loved looked foreign as I pulled into the driveway.

I could hear the faint ringing of the telephone as I reached the front door. With hands shaking, I fumbled for the key in the lock, burst through the door and raced for the telephone snatching it off the hook.

It was Kris. "We've got problems," she said.

I wasn't prepared for the scene waiting for me as I rushed into his room.

He was lying motionless, eyes closed, leashed to monitors, tubes, line, and electrical devices that seemed to fill the room. A cardiac monitor flashed coded 'stats' in florescent blips across a mini-screen. Bags of intravenous lines infused into his arms hung from poles on either side of the bed.

Feeling as if I were walking through a nightmare, I moved to the bed and lifted the covers in an attempt to touch his hands and was aghast to see that they were secured by restraints.

Struggling with my emotions, I listened as the doctor on duty at the time explained what had happened during my brief absence.

"We're not sure if he had a slight stroke or a heart attack," he said. "Hopefully, these measures," he nodded toward the various pieces of equipment, "will be temporary. We will keep his as comfortable as possible." He hugged my shoulders briefly and left the room.

Temporary.

Clinging to that hope, I pulled my chair next to his bed and contemplated how I was going to explain all this to him when he woke up.

His family, finding it impossible to cope with the interminable waiting for news reluctantly abandoned their vigil by their telephones in exchange for the comfort one finds in the support of a close relationship had gathered in the small waiting room outside the ICU.

Now they were filing into the room to offer their encouragement. Unable to concede to the finality of the moment they chorused words in quiet desperation.

"Hang on." "You can make it." "We need you."

But the insidious malignancy had become the victor over all the medical efforts, mocked our prayers and shrouded him in pain.

Alone again with him now, I leaned near his face and whispered, " I know you are tired. It's alright. Do what you need to do. I'll find you again."

I put my face next to his and drenched his pillows with tears. Stay. Stay. Grow old with me.

I was alerted by the broken rhythm of the cardiac monitor and the faltering hiss of the respirator.

His face was turned toward the window. His gaze was focused on vistas which he alone could see. Was he smiling?

I spoke his name tentatively not sure if I should intrude into his moment of peace. But the look and smile were not for me. He was mapping out his final journey. Other arms were reaching out. He was going home.

WHO WILL BRING ME FLOWERS

Nothing can reduce a home back to a mere house more completely than when it's primary occupant no longer resides there.

I wandered from room to room seeking comfort in familiar things.

Which wall to place the art we had collected over the years had been a joint decision.

Breakfast at the kitchen table and watching the news on the portable TV in the sunroom in the evenings was as much a part or our routine as was sharing the morning newspaper over a cup of coffee.

The sight of his neatly hung suits and polished shoes lined neatly on the floor of his closet brought painful and poignant memories and images of his immaculate appearance and attention to detail when he dressed for work.

The house that had once been so alive with an active, growing family now seemed to be an empty, hollow, vastness of space.

"Where do I go from here?" I asked the nothingness that enveloped me.

I lifted the wood caricature cowboys he had carved from their place on the shelf and studied them again. One scene titled "Bunkhouse Buddies" was intricately carved with the lined faces of the cowhands studying tiny playing cards and was my favorite. Other scenes told a story of their own as well. He had realized a latent talent for wood carving late in life and his work had been recognized by other well- known carvers and he had received blue ribbons at art shows. "No more of these." I murmured, returning them back to the shelf.

I felt myself swathed in a cocoon of despair and depression with seemingly no strength or will to fight my way out.

I pulled his empty chair next to mine and turned toward the window hoping to catch sight of the two mourning doves at the feeder that we once enjoyed watching in the late afternoons.

But only one was there now. Where was the other one I wondered?

Had he flown away in search of a more attractive mate? No, I reasoned. Doves are monogamous.

Had he been the victim of the cat owned by the new neighbors next door?

I glanced back once more toward the lone bird but she too had now flown away.

Feeling a renewed sorrow, I turned back to the window and noticed that for the first time ever, the daisies in the flowerbeds were beginning to bloom.

EPILOGUE

Some names have been changed.

I made no attempt to color the events described in this manuscript as other than what actually transpired.

Attempting to protect the innocence of others mentioned here would be a fete beyond my capability or desire since none of us can claim that distinction.

We were a fractured family that did not take care of each other and in failing to do so we hurt ourselves.

My older sister died in a nursing home curled in a fetal position unable to recognize her children or call her husband by name.   We remaining siblings did not attend her funeral services.

My brother and I have been out of touch with our other sister for years and have only a vague idea of her whereabouts.

My mistaken notion that in order to be accepted, I must first achieve perfection in everything I attempt to do has resulted in my setting unrealistic goals, overly critical self-analysis, disappointing relationships and perhaps stolen the joy of simply being who I really am.

Only my brother seems to have come out a whole person. This could be that by the time he was old enough to be affected, we older siblings had moved away from home and gone our separate ways thereby ending the jealousy and quarreling that had poisoned or lives. But most likely he simply had the tenacity to sift through the rubble of dysfunction and retrieve the good qualities (and there were some) and meld them into his personality. He married his high school sweetheart, Norma, a strong, artistically talented girl, at a young age. Together they endured the hardships and inconveniences of a stint of army life and considered it an adventure.

Discouraged by a failed working partnership with Dad, he did not return to the family farm after being discharged but chose to begin ranch life on his own. They raised a family of three children and I was complimented when he named one of the girls after me. All three earned college degrees and are successful young adults. He and Norma now live in semi-secluded retirement in a mountain home which they built themselves.

In my mind I sometimes still think of him as the towheaded Huck Finn of a boy that I once pulled around in our toy wagon but he can break a horse or toss a bale of hay onto the back of a truck as easily as if it were a serving of shredded wheat.

We don't always agree philosophically or share the same political views but we occasionally enjoy long telephone conversations swapping opinions and jokes and we are able to end our talks by saying, "I love you." As far as I know we are the only members of our family that can verbalize that emotion.

REFLECTIONS

I have not lived a perfect life, but I've been rewarded with a life of good health, rare opportunities and long days filled with more sunshine than sorrows.

I have not been the perfect friend, but I have gathered loyal friends that I hope to keep.

I did not raise perfect children, but I have been blessed with the opportunity to share the lives of three remarkable individuals whom I admire, respect and lean on.

****

I am in awe of the strength and courage Linda demonstrated after the cruel and untimely death of her husband. After devoting over twenty-five years of loyal, outstanding service to his country, Harold was shot and killed by a deranged World War II Veteran while in the prime of his life and just beginning a new career as a Federal Police officer.

Mike and Kris' faith and devotion while suffering along with Kelly through years of Chemo, radiation and numerous hospital admissions while battling childhood Leukemia are a matter of inspiration to me.

Jim's grit and determination that dominated his efforts to successfully obtain parental custody of Ryan and Megan in order that they could be raised in a healthy environment have proven that my pride in him has not been misplaced.

All three are remarkable individuals in their own right and may even be my ticket to heaven.

9 798888 729 1147